My Small World

Foreword

It is certainly not easy to be a poet. It's even harder to be an aspiring new poet.

Opportunities for the latter are so limited that it's very discouraging for anybody who wants to try being a poet. And it's a very sad fact that these opportunities are diminishing all the time.

That's why we at United Press are delighted to fight this unwelcome trend. Indeed, in the past ten years we feel we have been able to turn the tide of apathy which other publishers have shown towards new poetry, and establish a brand new bridgehead.

In the past few years we have managed to help 33,000 UK poets into print. Many of them have never been published before but we have been able to give them the encouragement of that first step towards recognition as writers. It's been a delight for us to be able to do this, It's been even more enjoyable for us to present cash prizes to poets who have entered our free competitions.

All the competitions run by United Press are free to enter, in complete contrast to the national trend towards making poets pay entry fees. It costs an average of £5 per poem to enter most poetry competitions. So if you submit three poems, it will cost you £15. There's usually only one winner, and all the other people who have sent in £15 get absolutely nothing. So the many thousands of failed poets are financing the few successful ones. And usually the cash prize is a lot less than the many thousands of pounds taken in entry fees. So where does all that entrance money go?

In running free competitions with cash prizes United Press

CLASSIFICATION: POETRY

This book is sold under the condition that it shall
not, by way of trade or otherwise, be lent, resold,
hired out or otherwise circulated without the
publisher's prior consent in any form of binding or
cover other than that in which it is published and
without a similar condition including this condition
being imposed on the subsequent purchaser.

A CIP catalogue record for this book is available from
the British Library.

Printed and bound in Great Britain.

Paper used in the production of books published by
United Press comes only from sustainable forests.

This South East edition

ISBN 1-84436-390-2

First published in Great Britain in 2006 by
United Press Ltd
Admail 3735
London
EC1B 1JB
Tel: 0870 240 6190
Fax: 0870 240 6191
ISBN for complete set of volumes
1-84436-383-X
All Rights Reserved

© Copyright contributors 2006

1itedpress.co.uk

is clearly proving that competitions with entry fees are an unnecessary exploitation of struggling writers.

It's been a delight for us to present big cash prizes to many poets and I have really enjoyed meeting and talking to every one of our £1,000 cash prize winners. I can state categorically that each one of these winners has been more than deserving. This certainly applies to Owen Lowery who received £1,000 from United Press as the overall UK winner of our competition which resulted in this volume of poetry.

When I saw the title of Owen's poem - *Ode to Billinge* - I wondered how anyone could make an interesting poem out of a title like that. But Owen managed to do it. It's a great poem and just shows what a beginner can achieve. Owen, who is disabled after a teenage judo accident, started taking a creative writing course at Bolton University only a year ago.

"I did a lot of research for my poem, in which I wanted to reflect the fact that Billinge is a small town which has to struggle to find its own identity because of its position between several big towns," explained Owen. "I didn't think a poem about a town like Billinge would have a chance of winning a big national competition, but it's my town and I wanted to write about it."

That's what makes Owen's poem so outstanding. His subject matter is a challenge but the result is truly impressive.

Peter Quinn, United Press

ODE TO BILLINGE

Above you, heaven and the seagull's call.
Before you, a map of imperial fall.
Between you and Ireland, no greater height.
The Armada fled your beacon bright.

Beneath you, miner and quarryman died.
Your heart caught fire when their bellows sighed.
You spewed up your stone to build our homes.
We salved your wounds with suburban blooms.

Within you, seams like capillaries spread.
Your slopes play host to the sleepless dead.
Inside your taverns legends spring to life
Of the royal blade and the robber's knife.

Refuge of romance, by Saint Aydan blessed.
Blind to all commerce is your ancient crest.
In this land of rainfall and black cloud burst,
For what the greedy fear, the poet thirsts.

Owen Lowery

Contents

The poets who have contributed to this volume are listed below, along with the relevant page upon which their work can be found.

72	Hugh Wood	109	Georgina Voller
73	Kirsten Hogben	110	Angelina Celik
74	Dennis Thomsett	111	David Kemp
	Lawrence Rich		Natalia Wieczorek
75	Tony Reese	112	Malcolm John
76	Christine Collins	113	Eileen Sheriffs
77	Davinia Wright	114	Aqil A Khan
78	Adam Colton	115	Ronald Finn
79	Stephen Jarrett	116	Yvonne Holmes
80	Betty Bukall		Hayley Watson
81	Christine Ann Gebbie	117	Alliance Rio
82	Danielle Burford		Ouedraogo
	Pat Sturgeon	118	Tracy Hassell
83	Angela Dimond-Collins	119	Derek Crowther
84	Robert Humphrey	120	John Merriman
85	Pauline Edwards	121	Ann Pendleton
86	Rowland G Blackford	122	Beverley Channer
87	Susan Langford	123	Leigh Grant
	Tony Graham		Phillip Everitt
	Alderman	124	Janette Patteron
88	Halina Scharf	125	Gemma Crawford
89	Colin Ralph	126	Emma Etherington
90	Terry Poole	127	Sharoné Maria
91	Betty Oldmeadow		Benjamin
92	Mary Burrell	128	Kaye Pothecary-Jones
93	Terry Reardon	129	David Wiggins
94	Helen West		Tiffany Huggins
95	Colin Jordan	130	Daniel Farrugia
96	Celia Ratnavel	131	Charles Kelvey
97	Valerie Ann Luxton	132	Lesley Hague
98	Hashim Salman	133	Claire Grayson
99	Hardev Anne Grewal		Elane Jackson
	Melissa McGovern	134	Emmanuel Sarpong
100	Carlos Nogueiras		Owusu Ansah
101	Vicky Thomas	135	Sam Mustafa
102	Rahim Shiraz		Randall Powell
	Moledina	136	Henrietta Keeper
103	Debra Cooper	137	Hannah Kelly
104	Ronald Hiscoke		Laura Clivaz
105	Laetitia Payet	138	Sandra Goddard
106	Miriam Mesa-Villalba		Angela Stanford
107	Martine Gafney	139	Diana Willis
108	Mary Leonard	140	Aeronwy Thomas

141	Mark Paddington	179	Terrence St John
142	Barbara Tozer		Pamela Laflin
143	Jessica Parsons	180	Robert G Bedwell
144	Ruth Tickner	181	Gordon Brenchley
145	Lynne Willis	182	Billy King
146	Christine Evans	183	Patsy Goodsir
147	Gillian Harris	184	Sheila J Leheup
148	Valerie M Bond	185	Avin Philip
	Roy Ransom		Julie Fouad
149	Julie Whitby	186	Jessie Fisher
150	Margaret K Brambleby	187	Ann Harris
151	Grace Ball	188	Caroline D'Souza
152	Brenda Wymer	189	Mary Millar
153	Andrew Carey	190	Brenda Gass
154	Peter Morris	191	Ann Smith
155	Joan Iveson	192	John Sheehy
156	Sherree Stringer	193	Paul Andrew Newman
157	Avice Land		Margaret Freeman
158	Idris Woodfield	194	Gailann Houston
	Muriel Sims	195	Rumi Begum
159	Susan Hoar	196	Jackie Nicholson
160	William Burkitt	197	Sarah Sidibeh
161	Katherine Daniel	198	Elena Tincu-Straton
162	Olivia Baker	199	Dipesh Tailor
	Jacqueline Hitchen	200	Susan Vango
163	Antony May	201	Peggy Day
164	Edward Breed	202	Peter J Marsh
165	Roger Heath	203	Tarnya Glover
166	Anne Whitington	204	Ruth Daviat
167	Doris Sidders	205	David Pennant
168	Dennis Harrison	206	Philomena Russell
169	Jan Green	207	Gillian O'Donnell
170	Norman Sampson	208	Merenptah Asante-
171	Christopher Lane		Douglass
172	Antoinette Christine	209	Les Pearce
	Cox	210	Hilda Casey
	Pamela Harris	211	Paul Smith
173	Christine Ward		
174	Ted Shirley		
175	Sandra Leach		
176	Joan King		
177	Daphne R Webb		
178	Lynn Capie		

THE ROSE

My eyes glanced upon a rose
Its beauty in glory an elegant pose,
Sweet bouquet ascending the air,
This rose is tendered with loving care.
Soft silk petals in delicate folds,
Colour vibrant, beautiful and bold.

Laurel Heath, Braintree, Essex

Dedicated to my friend Sharon, heart felt thanks for always being there. Good friends are there to treasure. God bless.

LIFE IN EPPING FOREST

Epping Forest is the place for me
An area rich with beautiful trees
That grace the land, it's very grand
You can walk through the paths
And under the branches that hang low
To find a moment of silence, a moment of peace
In the shadows below
The ground is rich with nature's spoil
The birds and the bees, oh how they do toil
The squirrels and foxes are having fun
There are hidden places for them to run
Now Autumn's here
The leaves have turned to shades of gold
Bringing bright light across the trees of old
And as the leaves begin to fall
You can hear the crunch beneath your feet
It really is a special treat
Epping Forest certainly, has lots of style
So come and visit from across the mile

Barbara Masser, Buckhurst Hill, Essex

ON THE BEACH

I like to swim on a beautiful summers day
Down to my local beach I go to find somewhere to lay.
I wait for the water to reach the shore
The waves roll in towards me, more and more.

I close my eyes and listen to the sea
Suddenly I am aware of someone near me,
A teenager with a mobile phone glued to his ear
In the other hand he held a can of beer.

Ignore him I though, but his voice is all I could hear
He was now drinking his second can of beer.
Into a light sleep I then did fall
I suppose the beach is here for us all.

After my swim I looked around
It was peaceful, nobody in sight, not a sound.
He had vanished with his mobile telephone
Once more on my own, I was left alone.

Sheila Ann Hackett, Leigh-on-Sea, Essex

CHAPEL OF THOMAS A BECKETT

Crumbling edifice, memorial to a man
Revered by his Saxon peers

Exposed, the stone laid upon stone
With thoughts of love, or of bread

Pilgrims' resting place, weary laden way
To absolution or to dread

Mason laboured, worked by sun
Rain gathered legends of saintly man of flesh

Priestly order composed the frame of sorrows
For a nationhood's remains

Raised up by men, cut down by nature's rage
And histories enlightened age

Saint or sinner? Rome or Rex?
Stones are silent as the men that laid them

James Goodsell, Brentwood, Essex

THIS IS PARADISE

Enter Bradbury House, residence for retired
Salvation Army Officers
Walk into their magnificent garden
Having colourful flowers, laid to lawn
Artistically calm. Serene atmosphere
Centralised. A decorative stone waterfall
Figurines holding an upturned umbrella

Friends of Bradbury turn it into 'Palm Court Hotel'
Adorning the area, umbrellas, tables, chairs
Individual place settings, crockery, napkins
Live piano, violin playing to residents, friends
People will say we're in love
The Queen's favourite played tunes by Gershwin, enthral

Gentle breezes cool the humidity
Tea, sandwiches, cakes, served by bright eyed ladies
Smartly dressed, the caring staff
A shady, peaceful paradise under the
Trestled grapevine
Love, faith, charity, administered
The greatest of all is love

Patricia Turpin, Wickford, Essex

Born in Aberdeen, **Patricia Turpin** has interests including
watercolour painting, dancing, drama and croquet. " I start-
ed writing poetry in 1992, inspired by my love of words," she
explained. "My work is influenced by people and nature and
I would describe my style as descriptive. I would like to be
remembered as someone who loved life." Patricia works as a
nurse and has an ambition to have a book of her own poems
published. She is a widow with two daughters and a son and
the person she would most like to meet is the actor David
Jason. "I have written a short story and many poems," she
added.

CHELMSFORD

Chelmsford is a market town
It should have city status
For twenty years I lived there
I moved from north to south in 1980
Lancashire to Essex
My children went to school
Every day, every week was full
Life was great for all of us
We travelled everywhere by bus
Shopping, cinema, bowling, eating out and
A great market, there's no doubt

Five years ago we moved away
From inland to coast
And what do we miss the most? The shops!
But no problem, the Diamond and X30 buses
Can take us on our way
They run on the hour, all through the day
Back to Chelmsford, in hail, rain or shine
Retail therapy will do just fine

Mary Jo Clayton, Thorpe Bay, Essex

MY SOUTHEND

Shops run down empty, sad,
Everything here is not all bad.
New pavements to walk, somewhere to sit.
Eat fish and chips, look at the pier,
They'll repair it soon, I hear
Adventure Island is a lot of fun,
for Mums and Dads and the little ones
Take a boat trip out to sea (see).
Southend from afar, in all its beauty
When you return you can spend all your money,
In the arcades, if it isn't sunny
Eat alfresco at cafes galore,
Walk down the 'Golden Mile' to see once more
The famous 'Dome' the Kursaal no less,
Reminds us of a bygone age
No dancing now, bingo and blackjack, gambling is the rage
As evening comes disco abound, you can dance all night
To a musical sound, go home with the dawn.
Walk up the High Street, where shops are forlorn.
And litter adorns, that's Southend on Sea
It's home to me. And a new university.

Joy Bufton, Southend on Sea, Essex

BURNTWOOD

The caress of the gentle breezes in springtime,
That puts us all at ease.
When tension floats away,
But returns to bondage in human kind.
As the river meanders along,
Like the blood that oozes from the cut.
The hidden treasures of the long lost prince,
Emerge as if from nowhere.
The secret behind the truth,
With the temptation so unbearable.
Hidden from the innocent,
But now revealed worldwide.

Shaajishiri Kanagasabapathy, Essex

ESSEX/SUFFOLK BORDER

The Anglian light shines strangely in the sky,
The translucence inspired Constable,
And many artists sketching, walking by,
Watching the Stour and Deben flow to sea.
We have our country ways, much stays the same,
The school concert, carols in the church,
The children glow and play nativity
The villagers are friendly, fields are tilled;
But as I walk across the vale and ramble with my dog
Beside the river banks
There's paper, plastic, discarded tins of coke
To indicate the changes in the rural scene,
Although we try to keep it as its always been
An area of beauty, a good place to live.
We've had a ram raid on our village shop,
Its not all perfect but its very true
Traditions, hope, security shines through.

Gay Burfield, Dedham, Essex

RURAL/URBAN BRAINTREE

A tranquil place, a quiet spot
My town's streets they are not,
Stand for a moment let your imagination run wild
Close your eyes, dream like a child,
Do this away from the town's noise
Sit on a bench by the fountain regain your poise,
Sit still, eyes closed and listen
Your dream like state will soon glisten,
Try it, Sunday morning early,
Before the air is covered in a shroud,
With smells and noises that come with a crowd.
It's hard to think it's the middle of town
Where nature can present a beautiful gown,
Move from the bench, walk to the flitch way
Our nature walk, will make your day,
Savour the trees, wild plants,
Scenery and this peaceful time,
All is available along the old railway line.
This area of tranquillity, ours for free
Relaxes and rejuvenates, that's the key,
Why our town is great and some
I hope this inspires many visitors to come.

Patricia Clark, Braintree, Essex

SWIMMING

Swimming is good for you, so they say,
I'll tell you what happened the other day.
We went for a dip, at our local baths,
To relax after work, and share some laughs.

Changing cubicles surround the pool,
A bit old fashioned just like at school.
A little tap on my changing room door,
My wife's dropped her blouse, on a soaking wet floor.

What could be easier, than swimming in lanes?
I don't believe it; I've got stomach pains.
I leave the pool, for five minutes rest,
Got to get back, to show I'm the best.

Gaining momentum, gathering pace,
I've just kicked some lady, smack in the face.
What a commotion, the lifeguard dives in,
She'll be ok, just a cut on the chin.

We leave the water, hand in hand,
Oh joy, to be back on dry land.

                    Ian Large, Chadwell Heath, Essex

REMEMBERING CLACTON

A seaside resort in bygone days
Expressed its flavour in many ways
Sandy beaches and a deep blue sea
Theatres and shows that produced a glee
A place that was so lively, with no time to laze

The evening theatres, the daytime, the pier
For fun and frolics were always so near
From the Capital arrived the Waverly boat
Transporting visitors for a day to note
Happiness aplenty to shout and cheer

Everyday a tale was born to be told
As Butlins saw stardom for many unfold
A stroll in the sun, a dance in the moonlight
Life was so good, so pleasant and right
Its heart, its soul so many was sold

And now not so vibrant, touched or seen
Still it's identity remains so keen
But as the memories grow longer
And the feelings are stronger
Clacton a miss for those that have never been

Karl Fuller, Clacton-on-Sea, Essex

THE ESSEX WAY

Lets go on a hike today
We're going to walk the Essex Way.
It wends its way through field and wood,
And the exercise will do you good.
It stretches for miles,
But if you're not that fit,
You only have to do a bit.

Through sleepy hamlets trapped in time,
Along coastal paths - smell the brine.
Through bluebell woods and fields of corn.
Be one with nature and feel reborn.

Flora and fauna abound,
Both in the air and on the ground.
And if you're lucky you say see
Foxes foraging for shellfish
On the estuary.

So come one and all,
We'll have a great day.
We're going to do it
The Essex Way.

Susan Carslake, Colchester, Essex

ESSEX

I thought that London owned my heart
But now Essex owns the greatest part
People think it's flat and bare
This comment is really not fair
Lovely green fields and houses with thatch
The sight of a pretty church spire you will suddenly catch
A very busy coast when the long summer days come
To Clacton to see the air show
Wing walkers and the red arrowed arrive the excitement grows
They're the best, everyone knows
Countryside and good shopping too
This county has much to sell it to you

Kathleen B Rentowl, Clacton-on-Sea, Essex

HOME THOUGHTS

Seagull perched on cliff top post;
Sentinel with steel - eye gaze.
The ever changing face of sea;
Gentle ripple brushing sands,
Or unrelenting gusts of wind
Tossing the waves to a seething foam,
And bearing on its surface then
Discarded bottle from picnic time.
Fading light, a darkening sky,
And in the distance the glow of lamps
Framing the lines of wooden pier;
With fragments of reflected light
Cast on the ebbing tide beyond.

Joan Ashwell, Clacton-on-Sea, Essex

MY TOWN CLACTON

Clacton is a great place
There's lots for us to do
No matter what the age group
There's plenty all year through

Have a walk along our lovely pier
Or see a show or two
Or walk along our esplanade
There's so much you can do

Our airshow is a must to see
On a sunny day
Have a meal in a restaurant
Or have a take away

Browse the shops there's plenty
Or just do what you wish
Bet you'll want to come back
So put us on your list

Jean Brooks, Clacton-on-Sea, Essex

Dedicated to my father-in-law, E J Brooks who will be forever in our memories. He is gone but not forgotten.

Born in Brixton, **Jean Brooks** has interests including crosswords, gardening, keeping tropical fish, craftwork and parapsychology. "I started writing poetry in 1991 when I was pregnant with my daughter Laura. I decided to write a short story for her as well as a poem and song," she explained. "I would like to be remembered as a mother who had many talents and cared for animals and people." Aged 50, Jean is a housewife with ambitions to visit Stonehenge and travel to Egypt to see the pyramids. She is married to Richard and they have one daughter, Laura.

THE LOVELY LADY ACROSS THE ROAD

Joan would always invite us round for lunch
And what a meal it would be
A thing to remember her by
How she'd always invite us round for lunch

I used to help her with her shopping
To carry it from the car to the door
Never again will she thank me
For helping her with her shopping

As I glance at her house
I see her wave from the window
I look again and she's gone
Back into her beautiful home

The tree outside groans with age
It sways and creeks in the wind
At night I hear it cry
Clinging to the earth so desperately

Mentally I cling to Joan
Refusing to let her go
I don't want to forget, I want her to stay
How I will miss the lovely lady called Joan

Ray Berry, Ingrave, Essex

SAINT NICHOLAS

Along the way from where I abide,
There's a wondrous church standing tall with pride.
The door's always open, the clock chimes the time,
The stained glass windows glisten and shine.

Inside is cosy and warm with love,
With heartfelt messages sent from above.
Christ resides in the centre of place,
His suffering and pain, etched on His face.

The holy water awaits patiently, ready to bless,
The church goers and sinners, along with the rest.
Empty pews line the walls, side by side,
Their peaceful seats, comfy and wide.

Outside the sun burns or the rain pelts down,
But the lonely headstones lay gathered all around.
Relatives go and visit the bodies sleeping there,
To show they love and that they care.

The round tower has stood for years on end,
While the door has welcomed hundreds of friends.
Saint Nicholas church is there for all to see,
For many more years, I hope it will be.

Amy Jarman, South Ockendon, Essex

'TWAS ON A MONDAY MORNING

Monday morning; Epping market
Ditched the car; nowhere to park it.
Missed the bus; just one an hour
Walked instead through wind and shower.

Everything from foam to fashion
On the stalls to spend my cash on.
Fruit and flowers, shoes and slippers
Clothes for adults, clothes for nippers.

Blinds for windows, cloths for tables
Sticky tape and sticky labels.
Drawing pins or drawing pencils
Handbags, food bags, foil, utensils.

Mats for cats and bones for puppies
Bells for budgies, food for guppies.
Books for bookworms, jam for spreading
Blouses, trousers, nightwear, bedding.

Finished looking, finished spending
Now my shopping day is ending.
Filled my bag, spent too much money
Now it's time to fill my tummy.

Barbara Levine, Epping, Essex

CLACTON ON SEA

Clacton is the place to be, we just love living near the sea.
In spring we stroll along the pier,
To breathe the bracing sea air.
In summer the children come to play,
And so enjoy each summer day,
In autumn the OAP's come on trips, for fish and chips.
Then in winter we get the snow,
With walks on the prom for a healthy glow.
So now you can see why we love the sea,
And Clacton is the place to be.

Jennifer Gowers, Clacton-on-Sea, Essex

ETERNAL NATURE

All in silence softly sleeping
and birds were nested warm,
in firm belief that all was well
in '87 came an untold storm.

Waking startled to a savage noise
of winds that raged till dawn,
devastation in rural Suffolk
was unfolding in the early morn'.

Oaks and others bent their boughs
lowly to the sodden ground.
Roofs, walls, chimneys, fences and
devastation was all around.

But nature's such a wondrous thing
and restores her beauty with hope,
new sapling trees now flutter their leaves
nature has won and man can cope.

Mavis George, Halstead, Essex

SARFEND

Where the Thames and the sea eagerly meet
There's a special place, you should greet
My stamping ground, I well recommend
Cockneys all know it as their "Sarfend"

Its famous pier stretches over a mile
Walk or train it, then rest a while
And when you've enjoyed the view from the pier
There are lots of pubs selling really good beer

The Kursall beckons, and the golden arcades
Lots of kiosks selling buckets and spades
Though, sorry to say, there's not too much sand
When the tide is out, the mud takes command

Ice cream, or fish and chips?
The estuary busy with various ships
Sticks of rock, or candy floss?
You are never, ever, at a loss

And to crown it all, some very good news
The locals all are cheering the Blues
Fame at last, a football dream
"Sarfend" now has a useful team

Mark Randall, Westcliff-on-Sea, Essex

HO CLACTON ON SEA

The happiness given to you and to me,
For coming to Clacton is how it should be,
A place to hear children happily play,
A safe place to bring them no matter the day.

The front with its gardens a sight to behold,
The shelter from sunlight that never gets old,
A place to come to get away from the city,
To miss out on Clacton would be such a pity.

There's punch on the beach,
And lunch if you wish
There's kite flying people,
And there's freshly caught fish.

An art gallery to,
With pictures that knew,
And all of this there,
Just waiting for you.

A pier with amusements with fishing and such,
A grotto is there a heavenly touch,
There's so much to do and so much to see,
Of this ever friendly Clacton on Sea.

James McColl, Clacton-on-Sea, Essex

BETWEEN TWO RIVERS

Sinuous, coiling, taking life from the tide.
Creeping, and turning, tumble and writhe.
Serpentine rivers, released by the flood,
Swallow weeds, and the shells, and the silvered grey mud.

Broaching, encroaching, consuming the land,
Once toiled over, claimed, now abandoned by man.
Ripples, probing with fingers that never can tire,
Buffet the salt marsh, disguising the mire.

Drowning the mud flats, a froth of white lace.
Covers the sand banks, disguises their face.
Filling the basin, depositing silt.
Sighing, retreating, clothing slime with pure silk.

On platinum mud flats, at one with the sky.
Sea birds, converge, echo a long lonely cry.
Wrecks haunted by ghosts, sink again with despair.
Beseeching the sun, for one last gasp of air.

Stealthily, silently, snaking back to the sea
Diffusing the light, now the tide is set free.
Pink clouds, suspended, streak the span of the sky,
Reflect a mauve pallet, till the moon drifts on high.

Andrea Allen, Chelmsford, Essex

EASTWOOD

Friendly faces, neat gardens, green parks and tall trees,
Local shops filled with the smell of baking bread scent the
breeze,
Our beautiful church steeped in history for all to see,
Just some of the reasons why Eastwood is the place to be.
Good neighbours, pretty houses, long walks to the woods,
Supermarkets filled, so many different goods,
Take a bus to the town centre, or drive to the sea,
So many good reasons Eastwood is the place for me.

Pam Farley, Leigh-on-Sea, Essex

THE BROADWAY

Bang in the middle of Barking town centre
Your sure to enjoy it as soon as you enter
Recently re-opened in December
Your sure to have a night to remember

Whether you see a panto or a show
Its a wonderful place to go
The broadway's patrons include Billy Bragg
Get down there on comedy night and enjoy a good gag

The entertainment is second to none
Take the family and have some fun
Barker the bear is their mascot
Comedy, drama, music it has the lot

In Barking there are many places to see
But its the broadway that fills me with glee
You don't always have to go up west
Staying local doesn't have to be second best

Tracey Tabor, Barking, Essex

ALDERSHOT

This poem is about life in Aldershot
There's lots of things to do
Here's some things what Aldershot has got
From beavers to kung foo

The town centre has no cars
So it's very safe
There are all sorts of different bars
And churches to follow your faith

The army has been here for years
The yearly show is great
When they leave there will be tears
Let's hope that's not their fate

To see the fireworks go to Manor park
In the month of November
To see them best, come when it's dark
It's a sight to remember

You can go to the lido, when the weather is hot
And have fun with your mates
Take a rug and picnic and find a good spot
Stay till its late, Aldershot is great!

Faye Radford, Colchester, Essex

KEELY

One day you will be
The place you see
You hear it said
Your child like smile
Your path was sad
I dare not dream
If only I could

Mary French, Dagenham, Essex

FATED IN ITS FAME

The pier has always been there
As long as I have known,
The longest in the whole world,
A symbol of my home.

And yet through age and mishap,
It's been fated in is fame,
Damaged by us humans,
But resurrected by the same.

It's had boats that have collided,
And recent fires did harm
But it still stands there so proudly,
In its burnt-out ancient charm.

Our pier will always withstand
Whatever fate's in store,
It's part of Southends history,
And will stand for evermore.

Valerie Fry, Westcliff-on-Sea, Essex

BAD

My local place is melancholia and mania,
Medication and blood tests because I'm B.A.D,
Alcohol anaesthetises and provides sedation,
The side-effects all have consequences of dis-order.

Television and radio are my local place,
Company and escapism help lessen my isolation.
Such intensity of feeling and thought are tranquillised,
Suicidal cycles deplete my strength and judgement.

My guitar, poetry and art hold my local place together,
Even when I'm falling apart, gravitating towards the poles,
I'm lucky to have a centre around which to circle,
Affecting my survival on the eternal sea.

Do not wish to visit my local place - there is no return,
Written-off without a job, left alone with only a phone,
I call a girl and invite her round, but she always leaves too
soon,
Like my car - I'm broken down, I'm so tired, but insomnia
rules.

I take my local place with me wherever I go,
Bi-polar Affective Dis-order, manic-depression, is my
universe.

Keith Martin, Westcliff-on-Sea, Essex

THE DAY HORNCHURCH WAS BORN

The name's the same but then you could not get there by train
For there were many fields trees and country lanes
Only a coach of four could get you there

It was said that Ned Horn's family went back to yester year
Where they lived the Roman way
But today there's buses and trains
But not many country lanes

There's a church that stands on a hill
And everyday it preaches still
There's a horn on its roof they say its proof
That the Romans did stay
The farmers used to breed their bulls for show

The winner that year was farmer Ned Horn
Whose horns were put on display on the church roof
And are still here today
The romans gave scorn
But that was the day Hornchurch was born

That romans wanted to build a garrison town
Then one day they went away
For the people prayed Lord let Hornchurch stay
And it's still here today

Robert Lane, Hornchurch, Essex

SUNNY SOUTHEND

Worlds longest pleasure pier our boast,
A marvel of the Southend coast.
On sunny days it can't be beat,
With ice-cold beer to cool the heat.
By train, or walk, enjoy the view,
That fresh sea air is good for you.
Most come early stay till late,
To take in and appreciate.
See sun drenched beaches all the way,
Their kiss me quick hats on display.
Fish n chips or mash n pie
You'll find a meal to satisfy.
Taste local cockles, born and bred,
The very best it must be said.
Then just relax, why watch the clock?
But don't forget that stick of rock.
There's bingo, dancing, shops to view,
And plenty for the kids to do.
Those cheeky postcards make you smile,
It's Costa del Sol, east end style.

Fred Ablitt, Southend-on-Sea, Essex

Dedicated to all the people of Southend-on-Sea and friends of our town and world famous pleasure pier.

Born in Westcliff-on-Sea, **Fred Ablitt** has interests including writing, fishing, inventing and motorcycles. "I started writing poetry in 1999 after a sudden inspiration. I discovered that poetry is the perfect means to express my deep thoughts and inner feelings. I would describe my style as uncomplicated, simple and imaginative and I would like to be remembered for bringing a positive contribution to the world and being an inspiration for future generations." Aged 47, Fred works as a plumber and has an ambition to further expand his writing skills and reach out to a wider spectrum of people.

SENTIMENTAL OLD FOOL

O little ones, my little ones
Will you miss me when I am gone
I will miss you more than words can say
No more will you brighten up my day

O little ones, my little ones
Will you miss me when I am gone
No more running with arms open wide
For me to fold you so close inside

O little ones, my little ones
Will you miss me when I am gone
What does life hold in store for you
God's blessing, in whatever you may do

O little ones, my little ones
Will you miss me when I am gone
All I wish for, as your school life you start
You keep a small space for me in your heart

O little ones, my little ones
Will you miss me when I am gone
Perhaps when passing your old play school
You just might remember, this sentimental old fool

Sylvia Adams, Wickford, Essex

Dedicated to the playschool, and the children of Horndon-on-the-Hill who still have a part of my heart.

EPPING FOREST AREA

Gone are the cattle pens of Epping's old-fashioned past
With the cattle market we all thought would last
The cattle were weighed and the sheep and pigs put in
pens
Breaking loose from their pens every now and again

Then to Theydon Bois I moved at a later time
Into a cottage by the forest which I thought was fine
As a youngster it was great fun
Climbing and swinging from the trees for everyone

Building houses of leaves as in autumn they dropped from
the trees
And family picnics on the forest floor who could ask for
more
Then rides on the roundabouts in gray's retreat
That was hit by a mine during the war demolition was com-
plete
The Scottish regiments lost half their men so the band
played retreat

Small bakers, shops that made their own bread
Now a Tesco supermarket takes its place instead
The drapers, a lace and material shop
Now even the old name has been forgot

Bread delivered by horse and cart
Had no choice but to make sure it was an early start
In those days we could be safe to play, not like that today

Edmund W Hockley, North Weald, Essex

DARTFORD IN VERSE

Victorian terraces in abundance
With gorgeous Georgian splendour
And Edwardian architecture still alive
Dodgy, dank, dirty Dartford
Rises up like a phoenix from the flames
From the ashes grows new hope, new life
No rubbish, no drugs, no louts
On the map
Bridged across the gap
A town to be proud of

Jan White, Dartford, Kent

MARGATE CLOCK TOWER

Born in the eighteenth century
Born to stand still
My name is Clock Tower
I am happy to be myself
I am never alone
People and agitation
Have been growing around me since 1889
Main road, beach, shops
Dreamland, cinema, casino, many amusements
All attracting people's attention
There is constant change
Constant renewal and constant loss
In the street, on the beach, in the people
All around me there is fluctuation
But I stand happy
I stand still
For that I was born.

Barbara Paixao, Margate, Kent

CRANBROOK IN KENT

This small quaint town is a true delight
With its tall smock windmill half painted white
This 19th century mill is a famous landmark in the Weald
It still grinds corn sometimes, alas not the amount it used
to yield
There are quaint wooden cottages along the twisted street
The old cloth hall and church where folk meet

Once this was a flourishing centre of the clothing trade
With the Flemish weavers and folk not well paid
The rich merchants from Flanders in 1430 made the
church new
But luckily left the old porch of 1291 and a few of the pews
The room over the porch martyrs were held captive you
know
Way up on the tower Father Time with his scythe looks
down below
People here are caring and have a pride in their town
You never see litter or rubbish around

Anne Churchward, Groombridge, Kent

WHITSTABLE

In the morning the sound of seagulls
Mournful cries remind me of sailors souls
Lost at sea
Not born as a Whitstable girl I love
Everything about it, the people, beautiful
Sunsets, that take your breath away
Sit on the beach, watch the tides ebb
In and out. It is so free.
Children crabbing collecting shells
"Is it a fossil?" they cry. Local shopkeepers
Always have time for you. Fresh bread
A lovely museum, so many places to see.
Lovely shops in harbour street, great fish
Places and restaurants. The harbour
Where fresh fish is caught and bought
A quietness. A sense of peace. I could
Go on about Whitstable town. I feel
I belong here. So lucky am I to have
Found this place which is so dear to me.

Jacqueline Redfern, Whitstable, Kent

ROCHESTER AND ITS ATTRACTIONS

Everyone who goes to Rochester
Must walk down the High Street
It is full of little shops and antique emporiums
Museums, bookshops where people meet

Cafés and bistros, you can meet a friend
Sit and talk of old times
Dickens' week is every year
And the place is buzzing

People dressed in costume finery
Colourful and puzzling
It always makes one feel alive
To see the family tribe

Going back to bygone days
And all the wonderful Victorian ways
Along the esplanade, the boats moored at their leisure
Any of these events adds to the pleasure

Iris Crew, Rochester, Kent

GHOSTS OF ROMNEY MARSH

In the days of yesteryear
When smugglers roamed the Marsh
And wild seas crashed on unbridled shores
The eerie drift the owlers' call
Echoed through the chill night air
For all alert with an ear to hear
Summoning those from afar and near
To the moon-splashed beach
With no questions asked

And still at night when the mist descends
Hovering silently above the ground
Embracing the trees and abandoned church
Wafting in a wraithlike haze
We feel the ghosts of the past appear
Returning to their smuggling haunts
Through twisting roads across the Marsh
And, if we listen, can't we hear
The eerie drift of the owlers' call?

Sylvia Sharp, New Romney, Kent

MR MURRAY

Mr Murray's always funny,
Mr Murray's always great,
He's not only my teacher,
But also a great mate.

He's always working hard,
Planning things for all us guys,
And he's always looking smart,
With his crazy, spotty ties.

All the kids at our school love him,
He really is quite friendly,
And his brightly coloured cardi's,
Are always very trendy.

Even though I've left that school,
I'm always going back,
To see the greatest teacher in the world,
To keep him on the right track.

Grant Friday, Sheppey, Kent

JOHN WILLIE

With piercing eyes not a hair out of place
Strong determination written over his face
A character you'd never forget
A born leader in all respects

He led his crew with firmness and pride
Ensured that they all remained at his side
The weakling, the winger and the bore
Were quickly cast upon the shore

He navigated his ship with undoubted ease
Through many a hostile stormy sea
Adversity and peril he faced each day
Overcoming them in a fearless way

His prestige ranged from far and near
He attracted respect and sometimes fear
A legend outstanding in every way
I'll remember him till my dying day

Derek Weeks, Ashford, Kent

SHEERNESS, MY HOME

I am an interloper, a Londoner I am
In 1968 I came, with my dad and mam
So different was the area, surrounded by the sea
New sounds, new smells, new people, a lot of new for me
I started at a new school, so different from my last
A system strange, but interesting, the old one in the past
I grew, left school. The comp, it was, back in '77
My kids there too, one left and one going into year 11
I have, over the years, grown to love this isle
All the memories, some to cry at, some to smile
It's steeped in history, some very famous queens and kings
Like Shurland Hall and Sheerness docks, importers of cars and things
Some people think it's in Scotland because it ends in ness
I tell them the garden of England is my home that's called Sheerness

Josine Barnes, Sheerness, Kent

Born in Isleworth, **Josine Barnes** has interests including crosswords, poetry and cinema. "I started writing poetry as a child because I enjoyed it," she explained. "My work is influenced by everyday things and events and I would describe my poetry as freestyle. I would like to be remembered as someone who was happy-go-lucky." Aged 45, Josine is a housewife with an ambitions to swim with dolphins and ride across the plains of America on a mustang. She has a son and daughter and has written short stories and many poems.

HOPGARDEN

This is where the hops were grown
Around three or four meters high
When looking along between the rows
You could hardly see the sky

Men on stilts attended them
They grew so thick and green
And when they were being harvested
A very busy sight was seen

The hops were processed into beer
A pint was strong and heady
You wouldn't want three or four of them
Or you would become unsteady

There is one thing for certain
You could find it wherever you went
And not only that, you will marvel
Such lovely beer came from Kent

John Robert Burr, Tonbridge, Kent

SHE WALKS

She walks
Always with a softened smile
Years are forced by time to flow
And yet she is still here
I hypothesise she is a widow
And I estimate she is childless
And I guess she is happy enough
With herself

I often see her walking
Where to?
Or where from?
I just do not know
We seem to follow each other
And have done
Ever since I can remember

She is always alone
But she seems to enjoy it so

Joanne Gough, Margate, Kent

DAY TRIP

Victoria. The train and our trip to Herne Bay.
Soot and steam, at last it's come our special day.
We hadn't much, mum did the best she could
For me and Cyril, who were being extra super good.

You can play on the beach, paddle as well
Put on your costume. Bee sting? Goodness what a yell.
In mum's old handbag there's treatment for ills and sprains
Yes, even elastic if knickers fall down again.

Cor, look at the pier, it's sure big and long.
That old steamer at its end, I hope its tied up strong.
There's a band in the bandstand and one at Kings Hall
Lots of postcards and trikes with ice-cream, I bet it's Walls.

So much to take in, I love this old town
When I get old it's where I'll be found
Come what may to the town and to me
Hurrah for this day at Herne Bay next to the sea.

Iris D Turner, Herne Bay, Kent

HOMETOWN

Beckenham that is my home town
It is also been the home of people of renown
Crystal Palace is near
Where great events were held
Kelsey Park, a beautiful park with wildlife
May queens on a nearby common
Things of history that have been let die
But there are many things still to catch the eye

Edna Mead, Beckenham, Kent

CLIFTONVILLE

As a child, by train I came,
To play on the golden sandy beaches here.
So quiet, a contrast to Margate's
Noisy throng. "More sedate," my father
Said, "than seasides with rowdy funfairs."

I live here now, it is even quieter
Now, as people prefer to go abroad,
Thinking they will find more sun.
But sun is what we have in abundance here,
In this now forgotten part of Kent.

I still walk along the beaches here,
The golden sand between my toes,
Warm waves at my ankles lap,
Taking me back through many years,
To the child that loved the golden sands.

Jacqui Aston, Cliftonville, Kent

THAT LATE MAY

It was a memorable week that late May.
The lanes were edged with Queen Anne's lace
fronting the May blossomed hedges.
And they had walked through brimming bluebelled woods;
picnicked in the Kentish apple orchards;
admired the dripping Wisteria on old walls.
They had photographed the rampant Montana
climbing fences.
For, once, it was a sun-laden week.
And they had talked of the past and their shared child-
hood;
walked by a lake, smelling the sweet mown grass;
and they'd eaten sandwiches on a quiet village green.
With one more spring, it was also one less.
Perhaps only a few more times in a long lifetime,
they vowed to meet more often.
Life ran by, work intervened, duty and commitment ruled.
The golden week was something they now spoke of
nostalgically, once a year in the winter.

Gillian Moysey, Sevenoaks, Kent

BROADSTAIRS CLIFFS

Standing white and proud
Like an earthbound cloud
I'm as white as a sheet
With the sea at my feet
I am the pale wall
Where invaders fall
I greet the stranger who comes in peace
I give shelter to the very least
And little towns and villages stay
Protected in my sheltered bay
Where sailors for a thousand years
Have greeted me with smiles and tears
My lighthouse warns, sailors beware
As it shines above the cliffs at Broadstairs
Charles Dickens enjoyed holidaying here
We presume he liked the atmosphere
A leisurely stroll along the sandy beach
Then up to Bleak House, trinity church, each
Remind us of times gone by
You feel relaxed, slow down and sigh

Trudi Burford, Broadstairs, Kent

ISLE OF SHEPPEY

I'm driving over this bridge again,
With bubbles of excitement, it seems insane.
It's just a little island, eight miles wide,
Only thirteen miles long at spring high tide.
There are, for sure, much prettier places,
Where I've been, with my well-worn suitcases.
Globetrotter now, a business man,
But I was born and bred on this island's span.

This is a place that time's forgot,
A comforting haven when the world's gone to pot.
Things change, but slowly, don't make your head spin,
I catch up with friends now, and family, my kin.
Travelling the length and breadth of the island, never far
from a beach,
Compact, unique, easy, everything within my reach.
I've enjoyed my stay, spending time with my mother,
So all that's left now is to go and see my brother.
You've been in this place since I was eight, forever fourteen
you are, see you next time mate.

Val J Cahill, Sheerness, Kent

SIDCUP

In the ancient name of Sidcup
Find the meaning 'flat-topped hill,'
Vistas but confirm the story,
Landmarks obeying nature's will.
Once a scene of farms and woodland,
Grew from hamlet, to village, town,
Glad some tree-lined roads still linger
Leaving Sidcup her verdant crown.
Cows, at one time, walked the High Street
Selborne Road embraced ducks and pond.
The old forge was often busy,
Watching children felt special bond.
Those who still remember Stangers,
With money wafted overhead,
Will, perhaps, recall these others
Cardys, Dawsons, and Wests, for bread?
Changes come as marks of progress,
Hard to believe, sometimes, it's so,
I just hope the best of Sidcup
Remains a place all want to know.

Eileen G Shenton, Sidcup, Kent

CANTERBURY CATHEDRAL

I class myself as lucky
To have been born and lived
Within this lovely city
That has so much to give
Right in the city centre, our cathedral stands
That many, many years ago
Was built with just bare hands
The men that built this church
Took many, many years
And gave their all in
Body sweat and tears
But what a gigantic building
Is standing so proud and tall
Lasting many centuries
The Mother Church of all
People flock from all four corners
Of the world to come and see
This work of art that's awesome
And to the end of life eternal
That's just what it will be

Daphne Fryer, Canterbury, Kent

MURSTON MOMENTS

Chickety-boom, chickety-boom
The eager train enters the station
As the whining sirens lift the litter from sticky pavements
Innocent voices play beside the cussing, swearing houses
While thunder clouds rap across the sleeping chimneys
The misty-eyed morning stirs to the diesel's drone
As gusts of cans rest finally, to landscape the gutters
Yet is there the sigh of a small bird singing
And a butterfly hovering over a faded flower?
A dewdrop world reflected, dried up and forgotten
Rat-a-tat, tat-a-tat, the languid train leaves the station

Jane A Chambers, Sittingbourne, Kent

WHITSTABLE

Early rise before school
Chopping spuds for chips
To earn 6p as a rule
To spend on Saturday morning flicks
Swimming in the sea on long, hot summer days
Walking the street, after tea
Watching beautiful sunsets in the evening haze
When the marshes are eerily misty
Rising early, bleary eyed
Collecting mushrooms, after a short bike ride
In the snows
Sliding down Duncun Downs
On a home-made toboggan
Returning home wet and cold
Drying out in front of a coal fire
Eating toasted crumpets
With marg of gold

Brenda J Austen, Whitstable, Kent

TEENAGERS

High Street Bromley, ten past ten,
A crowd of teenagers mob an oldie,
Whooping and shouting they surround her
In a rugby tackle they move her along
She's unable to detach herself from the throng
Where are the police, oh, where are the police?

Like buses, either not there, or in threes,
Police are never there, or seen by degrees
To swamp the place.
Poor old woman, what can she do?
Grin and bear it perhaps, as she laughingly
Accepts her grandchildrens high spirits.

The Christmas break is now going apace,
The festivities beginning to take place,
A family meal enjoyed by us all
And now homeward bound they let off steam
A pity no sign of police was seen,
To show that teenagers can be a dream.

Dorothy McDougall, Bromley, Kent

SIDCUP

Sidcup is a lovely place,
It's nice to see many a person's face.
It's nice to go to the park,
And hear many dogs bark.
Many people will sit on a chair
At the park, and be glad they are there.
Some are sitting in the sun,
Joggers are having a run.
The lovely squirrels are climbing up the big great trees,
It's nice to listen to the sound of the bees.
Children are making some noise with their toys,
There is the swimming pool which is always so full.
So many exercises to do in the gym,
I'm sure it will make you slim.
Then there's the church with many people there,
They have many clothes to wear.
Nightschool, so many subjects to do, if only you knew.
I'm glad I live here, and being so near.

Verna Western, Sidcup, Kent

Born in Barnet, **Verna Western** has interests including
animals, poetry and the theatre. "I started writing after the
death of my mother in 2003. I was very close to her and
had many thoughts and feelings to express," she remarked.
"My work is influenced by people, places and animals and I
would describe my style as spontaneous. I would like to be
remembered as someone who brought happiness to others
through my poetry," Aged 44, Verna works as a carer and
has an ambition to have one of her poems published.

THE LAST END?

Our bowls club they are trying to take away,
With a road that has no right of way.

Day after day all our members say,
Please, please go away and let us stay.

Lots of people meet in the hall,
Not just for bowls, but snooker, darts and pool.

Petitions are written for us to sign,
Hundreds of names, we'll make them whine.

We argue and say, we have been here since 1924,
No way are we going to be shown the door.

Not only us, Ashford Rail Bowls Club is being torn apart,
But houses, shops and business parks.

Come a day when we hope to relax,
To play on the green with our woods and jacks.

Susan Smith, Ashford, Kent

THE BELLS OF ST PETERS

Like an audible beacon
You ring out, striking and clear
Each quarter of each hour
Day and night, whatever the season
Whether welcoming me home
Or during a stormy tempest
Whilst overseeing cricket on the green
Or standing sentinel
Over a snowy landscape
A reassuring presence
In this world of speed and change

Ian M Tudball, Tunbridge Wells, Kent

BETWEEN A SHIP AND A BRIDGE

We've got a sunken ship off shore
Still full of ammunition.
It's bound to blow one day we're told
By men of erudition.
And all this little Isle of ours,
And all of us will go.
We should be trembling in our shoes,
Not act like we don't know.
We ought to pack our bags and leave,
But wait, the word goes round,
Another expert says don't fear,
Those bombs are safe and sound.
We Islanders just shrug,
"Well, let them have their fun," we say.
"The bridge is up, the roads are jammed,
We can't leave anyway!"

Mary vanDyke, Sheerness, Kent

FATHER UNKNOWN

Although I never knew you
I think you did know me
But I have no memories of sitting on your knee
Listening to bed-time stories or watching Jackanory

I wonder did you like music?
Fast cars, good food
Did you fly into a mood
When things were not so good?

So many questions left unanswered
That I would love to ask
But I must hide behind the mask
Of not caring who or what my father was
But the pain will always be
As deep and dark as the unfathomable sea.

Sue Williams, Gillingham, Kent

AROUND WHERE I AM

Along with my dogs to my garden I go
Where I reap the food for my family at home
The earth is rich where potatoes grow
The grass smells sweet when it is time to mow
Where I am the wind so quick
Salt air so good it makes life tick
Aeroplanes above me roar
From the little airfield, a mile or more
There is a little wood across from me
Where birds sing among the trees
To the east I see a large grey cloud,
Or is it the power station so big and proud
Flat beaches and sand dunes are to the west
Where young people play and old folk rest
Potting around, digging here and there
Working for pleasure is so rare
It is getting warm so time for tea
A drink for the dogs, and a cuppa for me
A bit more work 'til home I march
To my house in Lydd, on the Romney Marsh

Michael Peirson, Romney Marsh, Kent

THE HOMECOMING

A drowsy wasp beats upon the window pane,
As the chill wind thunders across the roof.
Winter Jasmine dances wildly against the wall,
As I see you stumble over the ploughed field,
You wave your hat wildly, and begin to shout,
The wind whipping the greeting from your mouth.
Your coarse brown coat now hangs inside the door,
And a warming log fire awaits your praise.
We watch each other as we share some food,
Revelling in our silent, loving bond.
The house grows dim, together we lay down
When mice begin their night time scurries.

But today, you slam the car door
Being late, you moan about the rest.
You ate earlier, so I'll not bother
I watch the television, and take a bath,
Then, finally, watch some more.
Now separately we climb the stairs
It's painful to admit, this time around,
Our home is not where our hearts lie.

Lynn Leigh, Dover, Kent

THE PEOPLE'S PARK

In Saxon times it was known as the Moot
A place for meetings and fairs of great repute,
It was given by King Edward to a baron as reward
For loyalty and service to his noble lord,
In those early days Mote Manor was extensive and grand
Fed by the River Len with much fertile land,
Where mighty oaks and many fine deer
Were reflected in waters of a pool crystal clear,
There was a proud Tudor mansion, the finest seen
With ornate chimneys and great lawns of green.
When owned by the Marshams for two hundred years
The lake was enlarged, must keep up with the peers!
And to honour the Lord Lieutenant, their patron royal
The volunteers of Kent erected the pavilion tall,
But later, with no heir apparent the estate was sold
To be used for farming and housing, for all to behold,
Though time has now changed, in its eight hundredth year
Mote Manor must face modernity and all that it bears,
The wheel of fortune has turned, great landowners have
gone
And Mote Park is now owned by the people of Maidstone.

Pearl Davis, Maidstone, Kent

SITTINGBOURNE

We first came here from London Town.
But the pace of life made us frown,
Accustomed to the city hustle,
At first we missed the rush and bustle.

Wednesday, the shops all shut at noon.
Everything closed, two weeks in June.
But now the tempo of life has changed,
The old High Street is being rearranged.

So, keep the smoke, dirt and grime.
Beggars and inner city crime.
We are near the sea, the air is sweet.
The local bobby walks the street.

Three children grown up strong and tall,
Fun and games, they've had a ball.
Judo, swimming, sport, skate park,
Orchards, farms, all such a lark.
Dull and boring? Not on your life!
Don't let the media give us strife,
David Badiel, "shut your face"
We've all grown to love this place.

Valerie Eastop, Sittingbourne, Kent

THE WAR MEMORIAL

The war memorial stands bathed in light
From the winter setting sun
A cold wind blows round the memorial, for the dead
Long shadows reach out moving
And embracing the cold stone
Names carved deep within the stone light up
As the sun's rays kiss each one
Cold is the stone that stands naked in the setting sun
Cold like the men that are carved in stone
Poppies that were laid with thoughts and prayers
Now lie cold and alone
In the Sittingbourne air

Edric F Swindells, Sittingbourne, Kent

DESERTED HOUSE

The old house stands bleak and cold,
It looks as if it's very old,
The path with weeds is overgrown,
Hear the wind in the trees howl and moan.
Through my thin coat its icy blast
Sends me hurrying on my way quite fast,
I would like to stop and investigate
Just what lies beyond that broken gate.
Through dirty windows I would like to peer,
Wait, was that footsteps I did hear
Or the creaking of the old gate post?
Did I imagine that I'd seen a ghost?
A little old lady appeared in the road,
Did she live here? Was this her abode?
I will speak to her, I will face her stare,
Then I blink for a moment and she is no longer there.

Audrey Packham, Tenterden, Kent

THE ISLE OF SHEPPEY

As I walk through the streets of Sheppey, just my notebook
and me
I look around, up and down, and write down what I see
I can see the glistening waters, of the Sheppey beach
Gliding over the golden sands, moving in and out of reach
And now I come to the main town, and the big town clock
strikes ten
Busy shoppers bustle past, as I move along again
I walk along to Minster Abbey, with its steeple big and tall
The bells are ringing and there are people singing "Come ye
one and all"
I am now at the statue, called the Monument of Flight
Celebrating early flyers on Sheppey, including Wilbur and
Orville Wright
As I walk home I see the new bridge and all the benefits it
will give
I see the sand, I see the sea, I see the island where I live

Megan Gunn, Sheppey, Kent

Born in Minster, **Megan Gunn** has interests including
singing, acting, writing, crafts and the girl guides. "I started
writing poetry when I was seven because I enjoyed reading
and wanted to write poems and stories for my family," she
explained. "My work is influenced by special occasions and
I would describe my style as light-hearted and topical. The
person I would most like to meet is the author J K Rowling,
because I love the Harry Potter series of books, and she is
one of my idols. I have written a few short stories and
many poems. My biggest fantasy is to act in a Harry Potter
film," added Megan.

GRAVESEND

I was born in this town; as a child I remember the sounds,
Of the Thames and its traffic, the water as it splashes.

I lived in a road with terraced houses, played in the street
and in all the houses,
with children up the road, we went to school alone.
Through a tunnel that echoed our cries, we'd run and hide.

I spent my summers in a stone cold pool, with a red hot
roof, you had to hop, to the tuck shop.

I heard a tale of this old man who lived in the clock tower
and he ran,
around at night, giving the children a fright.

When the new year came near, the tugs would blow their
horns and it was clear, the new year was here.

We have a princess buried here, she came from a land far
away, married a captain but couldn't stay.
Pocahontas is her name, her statue still stands today.

Nicola White, Gravesend, Kent

PLEA FROM THE CLOCK TOWER

Since 1837 I've stood here
Straddling Herne Bay shore near the pier.
Elegant in Victorian time,
Just as good now, though past my prime.
When I was Thwaytes-born, my face had power
Told watchless people the passing hour.
Everyone then looked up to me
Pacing their lives quite tranquilly

Three happy piers I've seen come and go
Burnt down, blown down, blown up, every woe ...
Nearby our proud Union Jack would fly
On bandstand flagpole, nobly high.
Panting paddle steamers once would call
Sailing mankind across waves to all
Shining places around our shore:
Southend, Margate and many more.

I've seen kindness, good manners and bad
But the greatest thing to make me sad
Is talk of fixing a fencing rail
To enclose my tower, I hope they fail!

Babette Cursons-Prior, Herne Bay, Kent

WHITSTABLE

What a lovely town Whitstable is, with it's
Harbour bustling with life,
In summer the people come flocking here,
The world and his wife!
Sunsets are amazing
They fill the sky with a glow,
Actor Peter Cushing lived here
Beside the sea you know
Life is lovely in Whitstable, the walks on the beach are a
delight,
Especially for me, I was born here and I will never take
flight.

Julie Cleal, Whitstable, Kent

KINGS WOOD

I am in an enchanted wood of great glory,
The trees around me hold lots of stories,
Howls echo around me,
I hear footsteps coming this way,
I see two illuminated eyes.
As it comes towards me,
A frostbitten chill crawls up my neck like a spider's
hairy legs.
The shadow quickly flashed past me.
Then it leads me
To a field of bluebells.
As they sway from side to side,
The wind whispers softly to me.
I am in an enchanted wood of great glory.
I am deep in the garden of England.

Lauren Clare, Ashford, Kent

SEVENOAKS LIFE

Green belt town, professional people resolute commute,
glad of work
Duty won't shirk, easy-going, stress hardly showing, in
their gardens
Flowers, and organic produce growing, practising
Craft and art, from indolence stand apart
Sport is not neglected, always someone for tennis, with rich
seams of teams for football with round or oval ball
To summer and winter tourneys give their all, although
Children well supported, higher education courted
For this the town is noted, then praises are sung for the
town's green lung that is
Historic Knole Park, graced by fabled Dutch, gabled house
Born of Chicanery, King's gift to a spying, lying crony
See medieval echoes in two breeds of deer, hear above lark
notes clear, these greet sport here has all the mixes
To sound of leather on the willow, rat-tat-tatting woodpeck-
ers tree grubs winnow occasionally their
Exchange for an anthill range
Folk too need to be fed, find their footsteps to supermar-
kets led
All life on an even keel, so Sevenoaks has a pleasant feel

Graham Watkins, Sevenoaks, Kent

LIMO TO AMARILLO

Thirteen today, and I'm not at my brightest
What ails me? Myalgic encephalomyelitis
Actually, it was the pits
Couldn't face school, was in bits
Least my hair looked the biz, viz, ice-cool extensions
Nice stretch limo surprise, Hollywood pretensions
Inside, balloons, happy birthday banners, TV
Me, my friends Cheryl, Vikki and co, mum and dad 'course
Luxury ride, Northfleet to Lakeside, sweet serendipity
Baboons! People like monkeys lookin', wavin', strainin' to
see inside the dark windows
My friends were like, well impressed, we felt like Girls
Aloud!
Home to a happy party crowd
Well-wishers, jovial, heartbeats ablaze
Helps, 'cause not many understand my malaise
Depression, chronic unwell feeling, headaches, fatigue,
cruel innuendoes
My entourage vamp me up hearty
And I was, 'gainst all odds, the life and soul of my party
Fourteen today, "Limo to Amarillo", cool laptop, I'm smiling
Good news, I'm going back to school, my decision, 'course
Oh my life! Top grades, I'm laughing

Hugh Wood, Gravesend, Kent

BRING A SMILE

There is a local comic called Dave
He is a terrific rave
Such a busy man he always is
So bubbly and more bubbly than a bottle of fizz

Always in pantomime in various roles
He crosses the stage with never ending strolls
His wit is so quick, the joke's gone in a nick
Oh bother I've missed it, I feel so sick

We go to his show whenever we can
So many artists turn out for this man
It's for happy holidays, for sick children in need
He organises so much, he does indeed

What more can I say? As children meet him each day
To them he is just a huge sunshine ray

Kirsten Hogben, Herne Bay, Kent

Born in Asheridge, **Kirsten Hogben** has interests including writing, travelling, reading and the theatre. "I started writing poetry about 25 years ago and my work is influenced by situations, friends, the media and my late father," she explained. "I would describe my style as coming from the heart and I would like to remembered as a teacher who put children's interests first and educated then to a high standard." Aged 61, Kirsten is married to Peter and they have children, Russell and David. "My ambitions are to help others less fortunate than myself, to be happy and to enjoy my retirement," added Kirsten.

THE LAST

The wrinkles gathering upon his face
Tell of his passion for this place
The tired look within his eyes
The loving words and heavy sighs
His heart, it breaks with anothers plan
But still he does just what he can
With weary stride and calloused hand
His temper restrained as he works the land
Life he sees is shifting gear
But inexperience is something to fear
This time he's known will be taken away
And in pictures alone we'll remember his day

Dennis Thomsett, Dartford, Kent

GREY IS THE NEW GREEN

I remember a time when all that I saw in Sandhurst Close
meant something
When the sight of the gas works
and the sound of a woodpecker tapping on a tree near my
window
roused my delicate heart.
When even the high-pitched murmur of a milk float
held a strange nobility.
But now progress dictates change.

Rip trees from their roots and lay concrete down.
"Grey is the new green" they say.

I don't see tall, distinguished oaks anymore,
just morose picket fences and nuclear families.

Lawrence Rich, Tunbridge Wells, Kent

A PEERLESS TOWN

My home town of Margate, with its spread of golden sands,
Its wintertime tranquillity, its summertime élan;
All these things, and many more made sense in moving
here;
Also, the affinity I felt for Margate's pier.
Since 1856 she'd been the queen of seaside fun,
She'd proudly stood, her arms outstretched,
Welcoming everyone.
How many feet had trod her boards? How many souls had
sat,
Relaxing in the summer sun, or hurrying to catch
A steamboat, for a coastal trip, a ferry bound for France?
Way back in Margate's heyday,
Magnifique, par excellence!
But, alas, in 1978, her final days had come,
On January 11th she was there,
And by the 12th, she'd gone.
Hurricane force winds ripped her apart in just one night,
Her timbers blotted out the beach, a sad and awful sight;
I've lived in Margate 40 years, through all its ups and
downs,
So I can say, in more ways than one,
Margate's a peerless town.

Tony Reese, Margate, Kent

ROMNEY MARSH

In a time-forgotten corner of Kent County
Lies Romney Marsh reclaimed from the sea.

Windswept beaches, shingle shore
A haunting atmosphere us Marshians adore.

From Dungeness Point watch ships sail by
The lighthouse proudly keeps a guardian eye.

Ugly power station, so stark and bleak
Fishermen's cottages, pretty and petite.

Little train chugs along, building up steam
Full of children, eyes sparkling, reliving a dream.

Tales of smugglers, the Scarecrow, hangman's tree
Fluffy white sheep as far as you see.

Eerie mists swirl o'er the marshy ground.
People with faces, but no legs abound.

Come join me on the beach, watch a Marshian sunset
A magical experience you'll never forget.

Christine Collins, Romney Marsh, Kent

ROCHESTER CATHEDRAL SPIRE

I am the spire of the cathedral
So high up in the sky
That people crawl like pins and matchsticks
When customers move between market stalls on fridays
It seems as if they are playing Chinese Chequers
Aloof and arrogant, I watch sweeps with brooms
At the Dickens May Day celebration
How much more finely crafted I am compared to these
ragged brushes
But, there are disadvantages
I can't just hop down from my perch to board a boat in the
harbour
Oh, how I envy the sparrows
Who sit on my long nose
They fly down onto the prow of a ship
Sometimes, starlings shelter under my scarf in winter
But they soon go, greedy for breadcrumbs on bird tables
below
It's a lonely life being a spire
Thank heavens for talkative Mr Robin Redbreast
Rochester's chatterbox
At least I can catch up on the gossip
While enjoying a hot chocolate and Alpen cereal bar at
elevenses

Davinia Wright, Sittingbourne, Kent

THE GATEWAY TO THE MARSH

Way down in Kent where the Weald meets the Marsh
And the woodlands roll down to the old ancient shore
The diesel trains thunder along the incline
From Ham Street to Ashford as in days of yore

But those who alight here, can wander at ease
Where weatherboard buildings line the main street
Down to the canal, to fish or to ramble
From Seabrook to Cliff End, its course is complete

Or follow fond footpaths to old ancient inns
In Warehorne or Ruckinge where smugglers did eat
Using Ordnance Survey maps, crumpled with use
For the first place they put on the map was Ham Street

Though you won't find Ham Street in tourism guides
And on Kentish road signs, its name is now rare
The village lives on in Kent's quiet corner
Where the sound of the wood pigeon hangs in the air

Adam Colton, Hamstreet, Kent

Adam Colton said: "I have lived in Hamstreet for all my 30
years and therefore have something on an affinity with the
place. Maps of the village once famously appeared on a set
of postage stamps to commemorate the bicentenary of the
Ordnance Survey. BBC TV's *Countryfile* even devoted an
episode to the occasion. As a keen guitarist, many of my
poems metamorphose into songs. There are details of two
acoustic CDs at http://hometown.aol.co.uk/ uklighthous-
es/1.html plus a book written with my father, humorously
documenting our lighthouse-visiting mission. *England and
Wales in a Flash* (ISBN 0954477103) can be ordered from
all good bookshops."

SIDCUP

As a new day is dawning
Sidcup is a town in mourning.
Not overtly, but underneath
As result of the death of Ted Heath.

Old Bexley and Sidcup was his seat
To retain it so often was quite a feat.
Years and years of total glory
For this politician, ever a Tory.

Try as he might, he could not match her
Yes, you know who - Maggie Thatcher.
But through all his work and toil
His Sidcup supporters remained forever loyal.

Whilst at the very top
He took the UK into Europe.
Above every other he put Sidcup on the map
What a shame he took such a rap.

It is only right that we respect the dead
But I am sure we will reach an agreement with 'Our Ted'
We must be loud and not speak in a whisper
That glorious Sidcup continues to prosper.

Stephen Jarrett, Dartford, Kent

JUNK MAIL, MY WAY

Postmen with letters, I've had a few
Now it is all up to you
Ring another bell
Let them go to hell
As long as I have it my way

Regrets, I have none
So long as I'm number one
I need consult no other
However ill neighbours become
Staying stone deaf always suits my cover

I did what I wanted to
Tried them to see it through, without exemption
Arrangements to them, I made no mention
I made my case and made it certain
(Mail deliveries may go for a Burton)
So, what have we got
All her mail, the ruddy lot
We've thrown it all out for today
And truly done it our way

Betty Bukall, Ashford, Kent

Dedicated to and inspired by, an elderly female tenant who was known to me in sheltered housing.

SITTINGBOURNE

The ever-changing town
Of which I placed my humble abode
Is changing past and present
To extend for it's heavy load
Of families and industry
And more traffic on it's roads

The old and new
Stand side by side
The young and old
Walk straight on by

It's delightful and charmed
It's however we make it
It's character and beauty
And however we perceive them

My town it breathes
For all to achieve in
My town, it stops
In remembrance of others

Sittingbourne is where I live and lay my hat to rest
So finally I've found my place my home, my town, the best

Christine Ann Gebbie, Sittingbourne, Kent

THE VIKING GHOST OF CLIFFSEND

The great ship that looms so far above
And is so old, filled with hatred and love
It's made from an old oak tree
Just beyond it is the deep, deep blue sea
What's that you see as you look at the ship ashore
A man in strange clothing but you are unsure
Whether he is from this time or another
Whether he is dangerous or just like a brother
He looks at you but it's though he cannot see
That right in front of him is where you be
Then he disappeared and in another language did call
Strange words and then you wonder, was he ever there at
all?

Danielle Burford, Ramsgate, Kent

WONDERFUL WALMER

Throw pebbles in the sea, listen to the band,
Watch little children paddling, often hand in hand.
Couples quietly sauntering, admiring the view,
They can see the coast of France and the ferries too.
There's a beautiful green where the fair sometimes comes,
A lifeboat guards the seashore, helping sailors safely home,
And pubs and clubs and churches and a castle to call our
own.
There's places where Caesar landed, tho' we're not sure
which one,
We have shops and great activities and an air of calm
abounds,
And in the winter months there's still lots of us around.
It can be very windy, sometimes bitterly cold,
But I wouldn't change this part of Kent, even tho' I'm old.

Pat Sturgeon, Walmer, Kent

DIGNITY

I cry out but you do not hear
I am numb with cold
Yesterday you passed-by
But you did not turn your head

Today you passed in your car
All snug and warm
But you did not see

In this 21st Century you should ask
"Who is that person?"

Shall I tell you

I had a house, a family and job
Now it has all gone
When you pass-by again stop and ask
"Can I help you?"

All I want is my dignity back

They say the streets of London are
Paved with gold
I have found nothing.

Angela Dimond-Collins, Orpington, Kent

SITTINGBOURNE

Sittingbourne recently has greatly changed.
The infrastructure is constantly being re-arranged.
Urban sprawl replaces orchards and farms.
Rural villages have lost their periodic charms.

We've now become a commuter town.
Many make the daily trip to London, up and down.
Strange that London was built from local clay.
Brick making then, was how locals earned their pay.

Taking bricks to London by barge on every high tide.
Bringing back the city's waste, to dump and hide.
Positioned, halfway between London and Dover.
Meant many coaching inns for travellers to stop over.

Paper making has been here for many, many years.
Doggedly still hanging on despite all the fears.
We don't use so much paper now.
Messages now, are by text or e-mail.

So whatever the town's future, let's hope it's bright.
But that will only happen if the planners get it right.
Let's hope they provide for play and leisure.
Then living in the new Sittingbourne will become a
pleasure.

Robert Humphrey, Sittingbourne, Kent

Robert Humphrey said: "I am 50, divorced for seven years
after 26 years of marriage. I have five grown up children,
five grandchildren and one on the way. I'm a Cancerian so I
have strong family values. I always enjoyed writing and,
since my divorce, have now found the time to return to it. I
enjoy poetry, it helps me unload stress. I always have sever-
al writing projects running at one time. I would love to write
an old fashioned sitcom, such as *Dad's Army*. My hobbies
include gardening, reading and going to the theatre."

EXPANSION

Houses are growing in Sevenoaks
Everywhere you look
They are creating enormous great mansions
Filling out each little nook

And when there's no room to spread sideways
They simply build on top
Adding another five bedrooms
When is it going to stop?

I'm growing increasingly anxious
That the sun may no longer get in
And, with all the extra people
The pavements will all be too thin

As for our once-famous Seven Oaks
I confess I really don't know
Whether, due to housing expansion
They will find they have no space to grow

Thank heaven for beautiful Knole Park
A sanctuary really close by
Where we'll all have to gather on Sundays
In order to gaze at the sky

Pauline Edwards, Sevenoaks, Kent

CRANBROOK

Did smugglers walk through Cranbrook
In the days of long ago
Were the Hawkhurst Gang their rivals?
Don't suppose we will ever know

Elizabeth the first visited Cranbrook
Stayed at the George, so 'tis said
The Town has a glorious past
Now, it is looking ahead

There's an amateur drama society
With Queen's Hall for pantos and plays
It also boasts a town band
For music, at gala days

Don't forget, too, there's a windmill
That has open days, to view
A church, a museum, a chapel
And plenty of shops for you

So just take a walk around Cranbrook
There are pubs, plus tea rooms, for a cuppa
At the end of the day you go home
Taking with you, your fish and chip supper

Rowland G Blackford, Cranbrook, Kent

REMEMBER

Silent sentinels
Guard earthly remains
Majestic trees
Stand in parade

The war dead
Pristine white crosses
Mowed lawns
Unwritten lives

Our worldly souls
Remember them
Gliding in glory
A touch away

Susan Langford, Folkestone, Kent

LEWIS ROAD FARM

Apples red
Apples ripe
Scrumping is my one delight

Apples crisp
Apples green
Belly full of apple seed

Coxs red
Cookers green
Doctor's gone an' been

Evening comes
Soon be done
Back to scrumping apple trees

Tony Graham Alderman, Tonbridge, Kent

BENEDICITE

A reconstructed memorial to you Father Time
Lording it over the parish, aptly over
The church clock at St Dunstan's,
A pioneering ministering angel himself, his echo
Chiming in Napoleonic captives to toil our hallowed soil.

You, you Pagan statue holding your scythe aloft
At our imperfect remake of your weathered effigy
Once questionably exhibited in Cranbrook's museum
For all to approve, I didn't
Haven't fallen under your spell yet.

We are parishioners all, held by your stare
Whether we like it or not we are trapped,
Aware of the sting of your sermon
As we shop in the Co-op for sustenance sufficient
Unto the day of your sharpened swish.

No new souls in your graveyard now
They closed it to newcomers after
The Second World War; after 1066 and all that.
Pity, 'cos we continue to need the space
In order to bury your bountiful benefaction.

Halina Scharf, Cranbrook, Kent

Born in London, **Halina Scharf** has interests including farm-
ing and spending time with her family. "I started writing
poetry years ago and my work is influenced by Beowulf,
Chaucer and Shakespeare," she explained. "I would describe
my style as deep but with humour and I would like to be
remembered as a good wife and mother." Aged 53, Halina
works as a teacher and has ambitions to visit India for a
couple of months and also to publish a book of her work.
She is married to Peter and they have three sons. "I have
written short stories and over 500 poems," added Halina.

GRAVESHAM

Ships sail on the river
St George's bells ring out
With people busy shopping
Is what Gravesham's all about

With football played at Stonebridge
Cricket at the bat and ball
Rugby, bowls and hockey
There's something for us all

Cascades and cygnet centres
Are places to enjoy
With swimming taking place
For every girl and boy

Princess Pocahontas
In red Indian dress
Looks towards the river
From her final place of rest

There are lines of heavy traffic
From Perry Street to Thong
So there's nothing more relaxing
Than a stroll along the prom

Colin Ralph, Gravesend, Kent

ORCHARD OF DREAMS

Today I walk west, to reflect on bygone days,
Of sunlit rays and glorious village scenes,
Of orchards laced with blossoms white,
Some pink, with harvest promise, bright.

Then, as I recall, the early morning dew,
Reflected spring's sweet spectrum hue,
And blackbird songs, filled the silent air,
With simple melodies, for all to share.

Now the orchard, that filled that space,
Those trees that gave sweet perfect grace,
Are gone, but human memory lingers long,
Of dapple shade, and early morning tunes.

Fat, red, sweet and ripe, the cherries hung,
To fill each picker's basket, with delight,
As they shouted with constant joyful glee,
And only stopped for brown brewed tea.

Perhaps tomorrow I will go another way,
To evoke, more cherished pastime dreams,
That cleanse the mind, in anxious times,
That lift the spirit, way up, heavenly high.

Terry Poole, Southfleet, Kent

THE ISLE OF SHEPPEY

Always in my thoughts, an island
Dear to me as the sun, for this
Island was my birth place, sand
And sea, for gulls a home.

The shore is decked with shells
And popping weed lies laced in a
Line among the stones, which tells
How high the night swell came.

In the light of dawn, when the tide
Deserts the shining, dormant banks
Of sand, small creatures still hide
In the now peaceful pools.

Trespassers descend to scavenge
On this temporary place, but the
Sea heaves back to seek revenge
And to wash the scars away.

This island has been my solace
Since barefoot I first touched down
And never will I leave this place
Until my last breath's drawn.

Betty Oldmeadow, Sheerness, Kent

Betty Oldmeadow said: "I started writing stories when my children were young to encourage their literacy skills. During 24 years as school secretary, my interest in writing increased. I was further spurred on by the work of authoress Katherine L Oldmeadow (my husband's aunt - published between 1910-1930). I enjoy entering poetry competitions; have had one published, together with a children's book *The Scooter Squad* ISBN 1-84375-187-9; available in bookshops and on the Internet. Since retiring I have completed a family history and find writing for children particularly enjoyable."

BLACKFEN

One day my uncle sat us down
It's time to leave old London town.
He only had a fiver then
He'd saved it up from who knows when.

Just right he yelled, a house not sold
We'll 'ave that one over there.
It'll suit us nice, I like the price
Two up, two down, is all we needs, I'll get a hoe and plant
some seeds.

Today the fields have gone away
And public loos have had their day.
Second hand cars is all I see
I'd really like to see a tree.

Time has changed our old Blackfen
I can't think why, I can't think when.
Fast food eating is where it's at
No wonder we're all getting fat.

But young and old, there's room for each
A coach could take you to the beach.
Let's celebrate and give a cheer
I'm staying put for another year.

Mary Burrell, Sidcup, Kent

STEPNEY, BOY TO MAN

Nobody prepares you for the time when your boys
Little soldiers, become young men

From that first step, until a walk or run
The first swim, no armbands, the first bike, three wheeler
Second bike, stabilisers, third bike, free, no hands!

Swimming clubs, sailor suits
Join the cubs, football boots, come on you hammers

Dance with your mum, all clean family fun
Trips to the zoo and Vicky park
Every beach, till it got dark, first to arrive, last to go

Glorious days, fun-filled ways
Don't waste any time, pack it all in
So much to do, so much to see, eventually just a memory

Growing taller, growing strong, plenty of friends, can't go
wrong
Watching their character develop before your eyes
Becoming young men with social graces
Pleasant manners, smiling faces
A word and smile for everyone

The hard work we put in, was just for fun

Terry Reardon, Tonbridge, Kent

HISTORY WAITING

Canterbury, town of mystery,
Full of wonder, full of history.
Dating back to times long gone.

In summer tourists come to stare,
To find the interest that lies there.
From far off lands they come to see.

And as they pass, we hear them speak,
In French or Japanese or Greek,
But do not understand a word.

Around are all fields so green
Where winding river may be seen,
And merry ducks go floating by.

In central place as is its right
Stands our cathedral's wondrous sight.
For miles around it can be seen.

Stretching its towers in the air,
Its bells remind us it is there,
God's special English home.

So come you folk from overseas,
And wander anywhere you please.

Helen West, Canterbury, Kent

BIGGAR BANK

At home on a filial visit,
I walk the shoreline path at Biggar Bank,
The west wind rampaging through hair and clothes.
Along the edge of the horizon,
A dull ship crawls, Fleetwood-bound;
No bright, romantic outriggers skim these waves.
A racing, tattered sky, all glare and shade,
Induces narrowed eyes and tiring frowns,
And makes me think of similar childhood days.
Ahead, occasional dark-clad figures,
Bent sideways to the wind,
Plod doggedly through the blowing, spiky grass.
Beyond, the giant hump of Black Coombe looms,
Once a volcano, now mild and rounded,
Black as ancient hide;
It forms the northern skyline of the bay,
And underneath its harmless, windswept flanks,
A worked-out steel town crumbles by the sea.

Colin Jordan, Chiswick, Greater London

ODE TO YESTERDAY

They have a story, the monuments and towers
That dominate the skyline; these blissful hours
Of yesterday, have a breath of poetry
And a flavour of the past, which has its priority

These majestic buildings and towering trees
Stand proudly against clear or grey skies
They never vanish, but graciously remain
As we step back and tide with time

Imposing boughs in a woodland, withstand gale
Rivers meandering, rolling hills and vale
Cottages hemmed in by fence, nestle in a landscape
Breathtaking, that gives the country a shape

It is history, to the searching mind
These chapters of picturesque heritage to bind
The journey between then and now, is infinite
For reflection, on the idyllic past and present

Celia Ratnavel, London

BUNHILL FIELDS, CITY OF LONDON

I watch the ghosts go drifting by
Past the tombs, the flowers, the trees
Bunyan, Blake, John Wesley's mother
And many others as worthy as these

In Winter the cemetary's grey and silent
In spring, the bluebells and daffodils bloom
In summer, daisies fleck the grass
And autumn leaves litter every tomb

The pigeons and the squirrels inhabit
This little city haven of peace
Where maybe the city elders strolled
And lovers trysted under the trees

Now city workers hurry through
All bustle and hustle to their daily stint
While I, who have no work to do
Can stroll and muse to my heart's content

Valerie Ann Luxton, London

CAMDEN PIANIST

I fell in love with Camden town
Since I saw you play Chopin
Since I saw your fingers dancing
Hastily, like the feathers of a fan
Which sent me in a colourful journey
Deja vu, in the city of Cannes
Festivities, music and dancing
All mixed gently, in one pan

I was passing cities and time
Joyous, careless, looking for tan
Until meeting you in Camden
Which forced a change of plan
Time stopped and future froze
No memories, no Beth, no Ann
I could not resist that magic
Who in this world really can?
She has all the charm and elegance
Since the creation of man

Hashim Salman, Camden, Greater London

DIWALI IN SOUTHALL

Silver stars sequin the night sky,
While in the distance,
Faintly flickering flames light the entire town,
The temple itself is a giant candle.
Its walls cloaked by innumerable flames.
Golden light spills over people's faces.
And shadows and light dance together.
Turning ordinary into extraordinary.
For one night each year.

Hardev Anne Grewal, Southall, Greater London

SWELL AND SPILL

On an afternoon by the ragged ring
It was once permitted far from the froggy king
Straight up stacks to staples knife, like and darting
Clear to the other mound betwixt the workers carting
Loads of finest board
Into the historic establishment adjacent the fjord

Mallard so many field of feathers gripping
Sunny expression frozen round the hissing vocals of the
sipping cackles broad

Tipping eruption smelling of summer juice drink
Cyclist bare course thinking
Direction two puddle or twist
Horse drawn pull the painting provides the apt gist

Why did you bring us here? And here within a click
Captured so minutely the suds roaring up so merrily thick

Melissa McGovern, Harefield, Greater London

THE PAPER DELIVERY GIRL

She does the same round every Thursday
And goes about her business with
The determination of a trained matador,
She moves cautiously, like a gazelle
And delivers the local news door-to-door,
Pushing her loaded cart up and down
The rain-soaked, muddy road;
She wears the same tracksuit every week
And always smiles when I open the door,
Today I greet her with a cup of tea
And Belgian sweets the colour of gold,
She hands me a copy of the paper
And munching her treats she goes,
And with her goes the hope,
But the craving stays with me,
Until we re-enact the same scene,
Like extras trapped in a silent film,
Who guard fiercely the secret hidden
Within its dark, convoluted plot.

Carlos Nogueiras, New Southgate, Greater London

THE PARK

I sat there at the top of the slide
Waiting for my mum to say slide down
Those were the days
When the park was full of joy and laughter
Children playing and running with each other
Now that park is not fun anymore
Times have changed
We've all grown older
No big slide to play on
No big sand pit to run in
All that's left is a few small swings
A roundabout
And a seesaw
It's not looked after anymore
Graffiti and vandalism takeover
I stand and say
Why do this to a place that used to be full of laughter?
But then I realise this place is
And never how it used to be

Vicky Thomas, Northwood, Greater London

HOME, WHERE IS IT?

Home, where is it?
Is it in the place I left behind, the place my parents left
behind?

Is it in the familiarity of a place I know?
A place where everybody speaks my language?
Is it in the warmth of somebody's loving arms?
Holding me tight, making me feel safe?

Is it in the memorable sounds?
The sounds I used to know?

Is it right here, before my very eyes, as I live and breathe?
Have I ever seen it, have I ever felt it?
Is it in the place I left behind, the place my parents left
behind?
Home, where is it?

Rahim Shiraz Moledina, Uxbridge, Greater London

Rahim Shiraz said: "I have been writing ever since the age
of eight, when I first started writing short fictional stories.
It was in my early teens that I discovered I had a passion
for film-making. I began to write short film scripts, as well
as make films, documentaries, music videos, adverts, each
time taking on a different crew member role. I graduated in
BA Film and Video at twenty-three. I still continue to write
short film scripts and have begun to write short stories
again, as well as write poetry for the first time and my first
feature film script. I find writing a great form of expression,
inspired by my own life experiences and of the people that
surround me."

THE TOWN

They say they're making our town
A better place to shop
Some think it's a good idea
Others not
We already have Palace Gardens shopping arcade
Now they are building the Palace Exchange
Our town, at present, is in a state
You have to walk a long way
To catch the bus numbered W8

There's parts of the town
That are all fenced round
Where this is, are holes in the ground
There are some roads closed too
But there's not a lot anyone can do
We will all have to wait
Till it is fixed
And that want be
Until the end of 2006

Debra Cooper, Enfield, Greater London

OUR STREET

These magnificent tree lined streets distinctive in all seasons
Laden with blossoming fruited boughs alike for one reason
To brighten up the neighbourhood as the residents declare
They are fortunate to reside in a borough that truly takes care
Participating with their own gardens to produce a delightful show
It is a pleasure to wander and observe many prizes in a row
Their beautifully maintained bungalows and water features rare
Add to the wondrous appealing sight as everybody shares
Here in this close community they are prepared to keep all neat and clean
There is no fouling of the footpaths and rubbish never seen
All take pride this is a communal task assisting one another
It's such a pleasure to wander the best kept street in the borough

Ronald Hiscoke, Waltham Forest, Greater London

HOME?

No hot water when I get home
You want to check
The freezing foam tortured my hair
And made it cry
Long icy tears
Fluin, brr, thousands of them
Dripping down my back
Heart
There's no hot water when I get home
Nobody hears
There's no hot water
My hair will scream
Hurt
In the secret of my chilly bed
There's no....
No more strength
Where is my home?
It can't be London
I would like hot water
Home

Laetitia Payet, Streatham Vale, Greater London

THOUSANDS OF SMILES

I smile at the smell
Of fresh coffee
In the morning
In Seville

I smile at the sound
Of the canaries
In my grandmother's garden
In Seville

I smile at the taste
Of gazpacho
In Seville

I smile at this child
I once was
Who never knew
The meaning of the verb
"To suffer"
In Seville

Miriam Mesa-Villalba, London

OUR HEATH

Amid our jungle of harsh cold concrete
Lies an island of untouched natural greenery
A wilderness alive among London's choking city.
An open space, a token place of peace
It's rippling ponds, rolling mounds and infamous Kite Hill
As old as the great oaks that litter the ground.
The place to visit to view all around
The London sites falling out of sight of eye.
Flying kites ruffle and flap, dart and dash
Like seagulls swooping, soaring in the sky.
In this playful place, this escaping place.
An eternal veil of nature and life
Fluttering birds, humming bees and children's shrieks
A haven for young and old alike
Where seasons pass and change
But Kite Hill and our Heath remain the same.
Calm and tranquil untouched by time.
Somewhere to breathe and cleanse your mind
Where winds blow free on a swaying sea of green
And we can remember how life used to be.

Martine Gafney, Kentish Town, Greater London

NATURE'S HAVEN

I'm living still in chic Notting Hill
Where parks abound and echo the sound
Of screeching peacocks fanning their tails
Kaleidoscope colours of courting males
Wooing their partners who shyly wait
Viewing the dance to choose a mate

Scampering squirrels scuffle by
Fluffy tails bobbing, their mien so shy
As they burrow to hide their nuts away
In store for many a rainy day
From bushes afar with poker hot eyes
A cunning fox observes his prize
Which he casually kills for tasty meals
Despite anguished cries and pleading squeals

The tall trees proud like sentinels stand
Observing these scenes in God's green land
Their branches sway as they seem to say
Come, make your home and we shall be
Always here as a shelter and lea

Mary Leonard, London

INSPIRATION FROM MY WORLD

I look for inspiration in the ordinary things
A tree, a dog, school children making too much noise on a
bus
A man arguing with a traffic warden, a mother scolding a
child
That sad looking person that sits outside Tesco in all
weathers asking "Can you spare some change please?"
Covered in dirt, hair matted, sleeping bag filthy
I would like so much to help, but I fear the reaction I will
get
Walk on by, as usual

I love the dark, the city at night is awe-inspiring
The radiant lights inside the buildings makes them look
like giant Christmas trees
It makes me feel safe, somehow
I like it best at dusk when I look out the window and watch
the night descend

This is where my inspiration lies, in the world around me
So much to laugh at, so much to cry at, so much to
embrace

Georgina Voller, London

BACK IN TOWN

The funfair here, back in town
Every year it comes around
Children playing on each ride, their mother and
Father by their side, oh what a fun the day will
Bring, excitement and enjoyment as they sing
Waltzers, spinning, round and round
As the music plays in the background
Eating hotdogs and candy too
Watching the ghost-train as it whistles through
There's donkey rides and coconut shies
Dartboard games and raffles too
So much choice, it's up to you
There's even a clown dancing around
Doing somersaults upon the ground,
The magician doing his tricks
And a big tall man walking on sticks
Then gypsy Leah the fortune teller
As she sits and chats to the toffee apple seller

Angelina Celik, London

Dedicated to my lovely daughters, Charlene Louise McMurray of London and Kim Marie. My loving sister Jeanette Barr and my brothers and sisters, the McMurray's of Hull, East Yorkshire.

THE OLD BAG LADY

You'll see the bag lady, every day,
With her face so lined, her hair so grey.
From the side of her mouth, hangs the end of a fag,
In each wizened hand she grasps a large bag.
She's often found standing around on the corner,
She looks so alone as if no one will mourn her.
From afar, she looks lonely, unkempt, and unclean,
But close up, the most beautiful smile that you've seen,
With clear twinkling eyes, that show love of life.
It's hard to believe that she was once my wife.

David Kemp, Tottenham, Greater London

MY LITTLE PIECE OF HEAVEN

They say it's dull, but they don't know
Who only pass it by
They say it's full of old folk
Who only wait to die
But pause a while and you will see
Its heart is beating strong
This little town is singing
If you'd stop and hear its song
It bids you stay, but they don't care
Who only want to run
Caring nothing for the gentle folk
Whose rushing days are done
So take your time in Bexhill
Hear the rhythm of the sea
It's a haven of tranquillity
To London folk like me

Natalia Wieczorek, Chelsea, Greater London

MY STREET, OUR WORLD

Every day, new faces, new families
Each step, fresh hellos, different cars
Everywhere, new children, unfamiliar postmen
My street, no different from yours, I know
But touching me like nowhere else
Skipping a heartbeat each homecoming stride
I am Odysseus returning after ten wandering years
The wastrel offspring slinking back after an indulgent glut

Passionately, I yearn for my ordinary, my extraordinary
street
Reassuringly, I seek mahoganied front doors, and discreet
curtain-twitching signals
From Bombay, Edinburgh, Peking, Chicago, perhaps
Timbuktu
Others quietly give testament to more exotic vistas outside
my street
Our worlds heralding voyages steeped in countless epic
verses
Here in my street, they pause, drawing breath
Anticipating timorously the hesitant steps of timeless jour-
neys
In streets without boundaries, worlds without fences

Malcolm John, Harrow, Greater London

MY LONDON TOWN

Piccadilly, Leicester Square
Hustle, bustle, everywhere

Cameras clicking, Abbey Road
Once was Beatle's old abode
All aboard big, red bus
Madame Tussaud's is a must

Hustle, bustle, all around
This is my London Town

Trains chuckle up and down
Big black taxis to be found
Sherlock Holmes lived in Baker Street
So do a million wannabes mate

Hustle, bustle, all around
This is my London Town

Regent's Park to feed the ducks
Squirrel looking for his nuts
Before retiring pint of brown
Oh how I love my London Town

Eileen Sheriffs, London

THE BOUNTIFUL OLIVE

Black, brown, green, golden and boasting
A plethora of shades in between.
This blessed fruit with Biblical allusions,
Found in abundance and cultivated,
All around the warm Mediterranean shores.

Unique with a taste of its own,
Relished by those who have it grown,
Harvesting and processing it in season
For a conducive staple diet with a tradition,
Descending from generation to generation.

Rich in vitamin E and anti-oxidants,
The protector of heart and its muscles.
Proven to dissolve bad cholesterol in arteries
If the fruit and its oil consumed habitually,
Substituting red meat and animal fats.

Available in countless varieties and brand names,
Cold pressed virgin or extra virgin olive oils.
Dress your salad, dip the bread or relish it raw.
Acquire the taste for olives and their oils,
The Pride of the proverbial Mediterranean diet.

Aqil A Khan, Greater London

Dedicated to Dr Taiyyeba, Taiyyab, Shaista, Sarah, Bushra Muneer, Junaid, Dr Fizza Naseer, Irfan Mustafa and Tony Quirke who I adore.

Aqil A Khan said: "I was born in Farrukhabad. Early parental upbringing followed by the best education both in India and England equipped me with a wealth of great ideas and writing skills. My work is influenced by prominent thinkers, leaders, poets and writers of the past and present, including Rumi, Khaiyyam, Iqbal, Josh, Aesop, Cervantes, Shakespeare, the great Romantics, the Victorians, Tolstoy, Walt Whitman as well as T S Eliot. The meagre collection of my published and unpublished poems is an outburst of my emotions recollected in tranquillity on myriad subjects reflecting our daily life. Through my philanthropic activities I want to leave the world as a better place."

GREENFORD

It's set back from the Ruislip Road,
Popular with locals for years so I've been told.
Like all pubs it has a distinct atmosphere and sound,
It's a strange breed indeed that uses the Hare and Hounds.

"Howdy partner," you're half expected to hear,
"What's your poison? Will it be whiskey, bourbon, a bit of
slap and tickle perhaps?"
Meekly you answer "No, I'll just have a beer."

A watering hole where you can congregate to catch up with
gossip and news,
Others seem quite vocal in sharing their views.

In the public bar that's affectionately known as the zoo,
The punters perform tricks while some throw up in the loo.

The Broadway beckons you to sample its culinary delights,
You are drawn by the smell of its many takeaways as you
transcend into the night.

The lack of quality shops on the high street is so evidently
clear,
A shanty town in the making I'm beginning to fear.

Ronald Finn, Greenford, Greater London

UNDERGROUND

Under the streets a perpetual round
Night and day motion with stereo sound
Driving a linkway through Hell into Eden
East Finchley, East Putney, Eastcote and Eastham
Rickety-rackety-clickety-clack
Green Park and Grange Hill, Great Portland Street, Greenford
Rickety-rackety-clickety-clack
Osterley, Ongar to Old Street and Oakwood
Under and over the ground level track
Near away, far away, echoing back
Dinning earth's core with a clickety clack

Yvonne Holmes, London

THE ONE-LEGGED BEGGAR

The area where I live, (or survive)
Is a bit of a dive
A one-legged man asks if you can spare change,
Somehow he got the mange.
Where his leg went, I don't know,
Maybe it was abducted by a crow.
Maybe he set it on fire,
Because his life is so dire
Maybe it ran away on its own,
Because its owner couldn't get a loan.
Maybe it gave up and died,
And ever since the man has cried
Now he has to hop on a crutch and jump
And when he thinks about it, feels a lump (in his throat)
"Spare any change?" is his croak,
His life is not a joke.

Hayley Watson, London

SYMBOL OF OLYMPIC GAMES

Eastern shelter of the melting pot
In Stratford station, the famous emblem stands
The 6th July I remember the vote
Oh, the famous Olympic Games.

London? Paris? Paris, no, London.
Yes, you rise grey and wise
Slowly but surely, we won
You blew away Londoners' worries

Yesterday so joyful, today cries
On the rush hour, a leg on the right
The pitiless hands had taken lives
A hand hanging on the left

Bring us joy and pride in 2012
Drive our children, our future fighters
Be grey, shiny, high and square, but be brave
Remain the emblem of sport and alliance

You stand where the sun rises
With your rainbow arms, you wear steel
Make me dream, give me the time and hope always
Be our bliss and strengthen our hearts so fragile.

Alliance Rio Ouedraogo, London

POLLUTION

Everywhere there is pollution
Cars bursting out fumes and smoke
Huge factories bellowing gases
Unhealthy for us folk

Everywhere there are trees
BEing killed by acid rain
It's all our fault this is happening
Why are people so insane?

Why is man doing this?
I really cannot understand
Killing all the trees and flowers
All over this, our land

LEaves on trees are rotting
Birds are flying away
There's a great big hole in the ozone layer
And I think it's going to stay

All this pollution is horrible
Please, we can't have anymore
All this industrial waste and paper
Put this in bags outside your door

Tracy Hassell, Enfield, Greater London

SOUTH OF AN ISLAND, ENGLAND

Here's a mix of town, village, hound, farmland and to the
fortunate few, sand.
Few find this sand, between sea and land, but settle down
on rough seaside ground.
There I lived awhile perhaps longer, like those I knew or
least their view.
Expressions like in verse or song bubble through window
pane,
Old and new which suits you.
Essential views from primordial soup to fall on ear of babe
and others too new.
On rainy day vocal hum of say is drowned of sound.
All things on land now silent both rain and day.
Did I misjudge what I know,
Mine or their cynical view.
Another thread for them or me to tread,
No leap to take, no hand to shake.
Just this primordial stew,
A well written recipe giving sustenance to shame or blame
A new game.
No spice but a treat perhaps to dawn,
An offering, a scoop to taste and enjoy, a formidable ploy a
toy.

Derek Crowther, London

TALL TERRACES

This area was country clean
Until Victorians came on the scene
Tall terraces were built up quick
The locals felt a little sick

They moved in gangs all over town
Tall terraces gained renown
The landlords smiled and shook their hands
And made a killing from their lands

They look so nice, I quite agree
Four storey piles of quality
Bourgeois pride puffed up so high
Tall terraces block out the sky

Stucco soldiers all in line
Standing firm through changing times
Reassuring in their pride
Tall terraces will never die

Renovation is the key
And they need it, constantly
Tall terraces decay in haste
They are an expensive taste

John Merriman, London

WINDS OF CHANGE

The church that faces progress
Stands foursquare to the winds of change
The market huddles round it
But the view's become so strange.

A thousand years have seen them
Both church and market square.
Lives and loves lived out there,
Celebrations, plays and fairs.

History spans those thousand years
With palaces and princes,
The Queen who hunted in the Chase
The dreaming church has seen her face.

Now it's view is changing
Bricks and girders rise,
New shops and bars and endless noise
They changed our town to twice its size.

But the church still stands dreaming,
The old market still survives,
Cars rush by in their one-way streaming,
People adapt to this change in their lives.

Ann Pendleton, Enfield, Greater London

WELSH HARP

Conservation areas scenic all around brochures crammed
with information forever to be found the Brent Welsh Harp
Reservoir
Is a pleasant place to be, family, friends and visitors enjoy
the scenery
Boats sail on open water, its sails boldly numbered adorns
their canvas
Excited to be a spectator. watching sails skillfully steering
Zig-zag upwards to the wind, following the radiant sun
If only one would capsize it would be a big surprise
because they never do
Speculating at the next Brent Regatta
Two flares, might steal the show
Torn bread scattered here and there, folks frequently pass-
ing by
Keep wading birds coming into view, of the camera's eye
Summer time is here again breeding warblers arrive from
Africa to lay their nests, constantly feeding until the season
ends
Emperor dragonflies transparent, long-veined wings play-
fully dancing
With the butterflies amongst dog roses and red campion
flowers
Hay fever comes once a year, I dare not smell the flowers

Beverley Channer, Neasden, Greater London

STREETS

Places, time never standing still
Changes ringing out before the year is through
The youth cling together for their identities to remain
Trying, seeking, some refuge or domain
Macho and bravery they wear like armour but not always
Does it suffice time after time, the youth pay the price
Only streets of boredom beckon temptation, side by side
With their sidekicks, drugs and crime
Some pass through with escape in sight, others, lost, run
That road not looking back to see places, time and
Changes never standing still leaving them behind

Leigh Grant, London

A TOWN WITHOUT PREJUDICE

This is my town which I've come to love
Sometimes I feel like I'm hand in glove
Its park has so much colour and life
With the serenity, you could cut it with a knife
We have no prejudice, unlike some
And are friends with all nations, never look glum
I know here I belong
Because my roots are so strong
I perceive an expression of wonder as I look around
The caged birds and those roaming free on the ground
Our scenic walkways are of a standard so high
You have to admire them as you stroll by
One of the longest markets of which I am proud
Is the shopping complex there's always a crowd
A fine art gallery to boot
We have the access, you just need the route

Phillip Everitt, Walthamstow, Greater London

OSTERLEY PARK

The treasured memories of childhood
Long walks, games in the field
Piggy in the middle and football
Saying hello to the horses and the cows
Down the long tree-lined way

Then rushing to the lake to see
The proud swans and squawking geese
All pushing to receive their daily bread
While the heron looks on aloof
Waiting to deliver his deadly stab

The mansion stands proud
Its Grecian columns elegantly
Drawing the visitor in to high-domed splendour
While the sweeping stone staircase has
Played host to decades of excited feet

Then down to the winding river
And the beauty of the willows on its bank
And round back in a circular tour
To the lake again and senses refreshed
You break the spell and re-enter the modern world

Janette Patteron, Isleworth, Greater London

To dearest Pooh for all the fun we've shared.

WINDOW OF HARROW LIFE

Casually I look out of the window,
Seen it all before...seems different.

Apples on great, upward branches,
Branches set against a lofty blue blanket.
Sway, swivel, swish softly,
Insects weave through wiggling, wavy arms.

Rich, royal, rust coloured roofs.
Gleaming, glistening, gorgeous glass windows.
Twenty, entwined trees scattered, patterned, dotted
Around light green, dark green, soft yellow fields.

Spectacular, superior, spell-binding:
Spirit of the church tower -
All lighted, love-struck, large:
Almost a living building.

Fierce, flying, ferocious fiend of fireworks,
Soaring, shooting, cart-wheeling, tumbling
Bang, whoosh, sizzle, sweep, crackle, splutter.
Through an endless, diamond encrusted velvet night sky.

All through the window...
Window of Harrow life, on Diwali night.

Gemma Crawford, Harrow, Greater London

RIVER

I live by a river and I watch it each day,
How it flows swiftly and then slowly,
I've come to think of a river in a different way,
I see it as a person and I visit it each day.

The fish are his friends and the ripples are his laughter,
When he flows swiftly he's playing and when he flows,
Slowly he's sleeping,
The rocks are his problems, the obstacles in his journey,
We play together sometimes when I splash about in him.

I love living by my river, he gives me water to drink and
A place to swim,
He is my place of tranquillity and thoughts,
He has cousins and children too, as he splits into
Tributaries and streams,
I wonder how long he goes on, he seems never ending,
I've come to think of it as if he just has not finished his
Journey yet,
The flowers on his bank are the fruits of his life.

So I live by a river and I watch it each day,
I've watched him flow and I've watched him grow,
He is my comfort, my joy and my friend.

Emma Etherington, New Southgate, Greater London

Born in Milton Keynes, **Emma Etherington** has interests including reading and painting. She is also learning to play the flute and piano. "I began to write stories and poems when I was seven. I grew to love nature, colours and scenery," she explained. "My style is free and comes from the heart. I would like to be known as an excellent poet and writer. The person I would most like to meet is the author J K Rowling because I admire her wonderful imagination and the person I would most like to be for a day is a gardener in Kew Gardens," she added.

N15

As I sit on my bedroom floor and ponder
I allow my mind to reminisce and wonder

In N15 you can easily find
Drug dealing, red tape and chalk out-line
Some people somewhat live in fear
Due to that gunshot they did hear
Today there's a poster on a tree for a guy that went missing
And another pinned up for sexual assault, that's the reality
we live in

You see me, I'm a born realist
I believe it should be told how it is
But in my heart I do have hope
So I guess I ave the trait of an optimist

Because as I look through the fog of negativity
I can glimpse that there's great potential
If we let go of those things that so easily beset us
We could grasp onto abundant credential

I can see that that time is coming
We're being sifted down to faith, hope and love
So my dream is that N15
Will turn and look to the man above

Sharoné Maria Benjamin, Tottenham, Greater London

THE HORNFAIR AT CHARLTON

Caressed by westerly winds approaches an inebriated band of revellers,
To Hornfair from Bermondsey they come, depleted by disease, the unforgiving leveller.

Dancing bear, jesters, pugilistic Punch and Judy entertain them along the way,
Passing plague pits at Blackheath, stench, nosegay, Black Death is ever present, never far away.

I'm Beth, a milk maid, never troubled by pox, I watch their approach, and it's rather bewildering,
T'is 1666, the fair is in full swing, wenching, ale, debauchery, drunkards start to sing.

People, people everywhere, stale sweat, man handled by drunks, the cuckold, he is everywhere,
The falcons become ruffled and agitated, can they sense something in the air.

Enough's enough, leaving the fair I look across the Thames to London, an orange plume of smoke's rising there,
I'm startled by the frantic sound of St Luke's clanging warning bell,
THE FIRE, THE FIRE, it's taking hold, oh God, they'll burn in the fires of Hell.

Kaye Pothecary-Jones, Charlton, Greater London

DAWN TILL DUSK

Silver shutter clatters up at 6:30
Another day's profits for the small corner shop
Outside sit Jim and old Carol
Just seconds away from the first drink of the day
Two cans of strong lager then they wander
Smiling at their new day
And the shopkeeper smiles and rings up his sale

Silver shutters clatter down at 8:30
And two empty cans lie crushed in a gutter
And Jim and old Carol
Look forward to the new day

David Wiggins, Stratford, Greater London

HARROW'S WALK

In the still and silent morning
In the stretch of winter's stay
Down a path unlade with footprints
Up the hill I made my way
Through a trail of tangled tree trunks
Past a church of standing stone
Near a wall of brick and ivy
By a yard of grave and bone
Cross a street of crooked houses
Next to a pub 'neath roof of hatch
Close to a school of harrowed prestige
With iron will and gates to match
Round a thicket thorn of history,
Churchill's wit and Byron's pen
Out an archway made of branches
And now back home again.

Tiffany Huggins, Harrow, Greater London

TRENT PARK

Walking in the winter chill,
As the cold wintry weather kills,
The misty frosty sun,
Shines until the day is done.

There we walk in the platoon of trees,
The foliage either side like skeletons alongside without any
leaves,
The road that leads to the point of the world,
Like the weaving of a patchwork that is sewed and twirled.

A robin flies high in the sky,
As I wave to the winter goodbye,
The beauty of the birth of spring,
That shines out to the world like a king.

For no more yet is the winter,
No more suffering for the cold chill that hurts like a splin-
ter,
Time for the sun to warm the grass,
As we roll around in it and laugh.

I viewed all of this in my time,
The wondrous beauty of life that loves to shine,
Yet God has left his mark,
In his creation of Trent Park.

Daniel Farrugia, Southgate, Greater London

DONALD BAY

You ask me where I come from, friend? No please, don't
turn away

I'll tell you where I come, friend, ti was a place called
Donald Bay

Now does that name bring a picture to your mind of say, a
peaceful cove on Scotland's rugged shore

And beyond, a nestling village lay mountain, glen and
heather-scented moor

Where from clear, cold streams a pleasured eye might see
trout and salmon leap the former leaping for a fly, the lat-
ter a destiny to keep

And high up in the lofty mountains where man (the spoiler)
seldom goes

The regal stag might seek fulfilment from the sloe eye'd
gentle doe, and do battle for her favour in the softly falling
snow

Ah, alas my friend, it was none of this, but I'll tell you is
you are interested to know

It was just a grimy little street in London's poverty-stricken
East End, in an area known as Bow

Charles Kelvey, Bow, Greater London

MY ENVIRONMENT

As a born and bred Eastender
My childhood was a lark
Playing bulldog on my favourite green
Or runouts after dark

Today the change is all around
More buildings just appear
Vandals, ASBOs and graffitti's rife
Old people live in fear

Has the place changed for the worse?
Or is it much the same?
I remember watching local boys
Throwing fireworks as a game

We played on fenced-up debris
Left abandoned from the past
Today regeneration
Gives us green spaces that will last

The mile-end park's impressive
So much better than before
The area's reborn to me
My eastend, that I adore

Lesley Hague, Hackney, Greater London

Dedicated to Tom O'Mahony, my soul-mate and saviour forever. Also Julie, Darren and Jackie, Leopold Estate during the 1970's.

LONDON SKYLINE

Stars illuminate the skies
Like an asteroid exploding into countless
Shards of brilliance
Escaping from the blackness and the void
Into a sight that staggers the senses

I am overwhelmed by the vast tapestry overhead
That can change the ink-black Thames into a vibrant sight
Reflecting out city in its velvety ripples
And as I raise my eyes and gaze at the splendid skyline
I see a city steeped in history and tradition
I see London staring me in the face

Claire Grayson, London

WHERE I LIVE AND WHERE I WORK

I look at the surroundings of the place where I live;
I see every day people and every day places,
The neighbours are quiet and the streets are all clean,
And those that we meet are friendly and kind.

Then I venture far off to the place that I work,
Where they are loud and indifferent, and not very nice.
They ask if I'm happy, in the things that I do,
I tell them I'm trying, but I won't tell a lie.

My surroundings are fine, it's just the people I see,
They speak different languages, I can't understand,
So I find a quiet corner, there I sit by myself,
For there I am happy, and write poetry instead.

Elane Jackson, Winchmore Hill, Greater London

THE PLACE I CALL HOME

In the womb of majestic and seemingly impenetrable
Ashanti forest
Lies Offinso, the region of my humble birth, the place I call
home
A tender-hearted mother whose children show supreme
affection
To strangers, even the strangest of the strange.

I can still feel the gentle breeze and the cold embrace of the
tender goddess,
The Offin river who meanders her way through the thick
woods
Down that little valley, stretching to join the Pra river
Before eventually arriving at the mighty ocean.

The voices of cocks and birds penetrate those ancient-like
wooden windows
Heralding the emergence of a glorious new day
Children are enthusiastically roaming those little streets
Compellingly immortalising childhood.

Now the moon is gradually unveiling her adorably bright
but ugly face
Announcing the nearness of the night
Disappointment found in the faces of folks who still have
more to do
But that is how it is, without the night, the day is not.

Emmanuel Sarpong Owusu Ansah, London

Dedicated to all my brothers and sisters, and the entire people of Offinso in the Ashanti Kingdom, Ghana.

LONDON LANDSCAPES

Carved into the skyline is a heritage of a thousand years,
flowing with life is the river, the cradle of our civilisation,
But with time and arrival of more waters,
Has our city grown.
Through ages of magic and men,
London has evolved to the rhythm of life.

During the forging of our way of life,
Excellence, perfection and mistakes
have all made their way through this city of cities
and enriched it with their grace.
London landscapes have been born
And forever will be immortal.

Sam Mustafa, North Finchely, Greater London

THE GLADSTONE PARK BIRDS FLYING

I saw flock of birds, in the local park,
Floating up in circles, leaving the earth behind,
Gliding in formation, up toward the sky.

Effortless drifting gravity on currents of air,
A truly amazing spectacle, wings spread wide,
Not flapping or exerting up or down.

Twisting, turning, bobbing, weaving in the air,
Fine tuning, making whirlpools in the sky.

they met no resistance, spiralling around.
Ascending lightly descending slightly,
Flowing on turbulence of the air.

Randall Powell, London

WHITECHAPEL, WHITECHAPEL

Whitechapel Whitechapel if you could speak
You would tell a tale quite unique
Whitechapel Whitechapel early at five
Not yet awake, not yet alive
Whitechapel Whitechapel later at nine
Barrow boys out when the weather is fine
Whitechapel Whitechapel where the buses run
To London hospital, I've cut my thumb
Whitechapel Whitechapel a historic place
East London's byway with a cockney face
Whitechapel Whitechapel late as nine
Out to drink the booze and wine
Whitechapel Whitechapel homeward bound
All deserted, not a sound
Whitechapel Whitechapel as the East End dies
To rest awhile till the morning rise
Whitechapel Whitechapel in all its fame
Still lives on again and again

Henrietta Keeper, Stepney, Greater London

Dedicated to my late husband Joseph and also my three daughters Lesley, Linda and Lorraine.

Born in London, **Henrietta Keeper** has interests including poetry, singing and studying nutrition. "I started writing poetry in April 1979 and my work is influenced by John Betjeman," she remarked. "I would like to be remembered as an honest person and a credit to my family and friends." Aged 79, Henrietta is a retired filing room supervisor with an ambition to publish a book of poems. She is the widow of Joseph and has three daughters. "My biggest fantasy is to win the lottery and my worst nightmare is flying on a plane," added Henrietta.

NIKKY IN FULHAM

Coming back from
Church,
I saw her
On the 14 bus.

I called out -
She came and kissed
Me -
My lovely domestic -

She then changed
To a 391 -
And the loss
Was mine.

Hannah Kelly, London

THE PARK

Technically it's called West Harrow Recreation Ground
But I just call it the park
I go to the park a lot
Sometimes I swing
On the swings
For ages
Sometimes I practice wheelies on my bike
But I haven't managed to do one yet
Someday I will
But sometimes
I go up my secret path
And climb my secret tree
And sit
And think

Laura Clivaz, Harrow, Greater London

MY TOWN

My town is large,
Its like no other place.
There are so many shops and buildings,
There is no space.
The town is so beautiful,
The River Thames put a smile on your face.
With the boats and the old buildings,
With the lovely flowers that light the town.
Full of grace when I go out at night time,
Put a smile on my face.

Sandra Goddard, Kingston upon Thames, Surrey

THE OLD HOMESTEAD

This house full of memories is where I was born
Now it's to be sold and hearts will be torn
For sixty odd years it's been in our name
But the street is so changed and nothings the same
This victorian dwelling, once our pride and joy
Not even the bombs of a war could destroy
Parties took place within these four walls
While kids ran amok up and down the two halls
The dear little garden, full of pets that we'd cherished
Lovingly buried after they'd perished
The old shed is still standing, where once we played house
Never deterred by the odd spider or mouse
The tiny back bedroom was mine all alone
In this lovely old refuge that I knew as home
It has witnessed much laughter and equally sorrow
Now it's time to let go and look to tomorrow

Angela Stanford, Croydon, Surrey

MEMORIES IN WOKING PARK

A name on a map was all I knew,
But now a precious memory for you.
I had no childish ventures in this place,
Although I can recall your laughing face.
Beside these leafy giants I see your little feet,
Pedalling round and round to keep you on the seat.
I see you stooping, intent upon the ground,
Searching for your conker treasure, shiny brown.

How we rushed to reach the pool, a river wide,
And year by year I watched you glisten from the side.
And then the day which seemed to come so soon,
When you were off, splashing in the blue lagoon.
Always through the tempting playground you would go,
And I would wander down the winding hill, so slow.
To give you time to tear through every single thing,
The little bridge, the slide, the train, the everlasting swing.

And thinking back I know my roots have grown,
Become entangled and nurtured with your own.

Diana Willis, Woking, Surrey

BROWN'S HOTEL, LAUGHARNE

We like our pubs a little worn - see -
No posh cocktail bar or fancy beers
They come in here from London
Flashing their money around
Making changes cleaning everything up
This is Wales, mun, not Soho
We like the yellow ceilings
And our fitted carpet as it was
It's like our lives have been
Steam-cleaned away
And all those strong beers
We like them weak
You can sink ten session beers
And still get home
And that jukebox they've put in
It's no joke neither
We all have to go down to
The Rugby Club now
For a bit of peace and quiet
It's cheaper beer too.

Aeronwy Thomas, New Malden, Surrey

THE WONDERS OF WOKING TOWN

The colour of this place lies somewhere between
Black and white. Viewed best under a leaden sky,
Follow the cries drifting from the
Exotic markets of Gaul, Rome and Mumbai
To the concrete piazza. Once there,
Cast your eyes upon the second seat of Wolsey,
Ridden by a plague of decadent rats.
Then across the square, see the peacocks standing proud,
With a fine display of granite and grey,
Flaunting their worth,
Whilst all around pay homage to such extravagance.
Beyond the centre beats the true heart,
Pumping a rich mixture that flows from
The sturdy foundations of St Peter to the
Domed palace of Allah,
Whose resplendent white and jade attire
Implores all who pass to admire.
Further still, seek the hand that crafts the Silver Arrows,
A divine creator who moulds dreams and
Transfixes men with adoration.
Will you wander to the wonders of Woking Town?

Mark Paddington, Woking, Surrey

MY HOME

My kitchen's like a foreign land
Things that always were at hand
Have disappeared, I know not where
The picnic basket now I find
Is in a cupboard
Behind a door
No longer standing on the floor
So now when I defrost the fridge
I'll know where I can find it

The iron has disappeared from view
Hidden among the drying clothes
A rose between some loopy towels
But smelling sweetly all the while
Of eau de linge
A present from another child
Who when at home
Delights to be
The daughter of my destiny
In that together with her sister
They rearrange the family

Barbara Tozer, Caterham, Surrey

CROYDON

Frantic shoppers
Slowly breathing in the muggy air as you enter the centre
Shoppers scampering to find the best sale items

Pavements decorated with neglected chewing gum
Bundles of litter in ever nook and cranny
Rude boys picking a fight with a drunk

The lonely wind breezing against sweating faces
Champions scoring the winning goal in a bet
Crystal Palace stadium madness

Tall sky scrapers scratching the sky and tickling the clouds
Itching the hungry belly of heaven
Ready to catch the sun

Traffic wardens weaving in and out of cars ready to pounce
Queues destroyed as uniformed kids push their way home
Red and white trams slithering in and out of creeks in the
jungle of Croydon

Staring from windows at the urban kingdom

Jessica Parsons, Croydon, Surrey

DAPHNE AND FRED

Daphne and Fred live next door,
They have been there forever more.
Their privet hedge grows forever green,
Together they make the perfect team.
Daphne and Fred live next door.

Daphne and Fred are always on hand,
To listen and understand.
Troubles and woes of all around,
To give advice solid and sound.
Daphne and Fred live next door.

Daphne and Fred do not sit around,
They can always be found.
Working hard for the Red Cross,
Who without them would know a loss.
Daphne and Fred live next door.

In the war while Fred was at sea,
Daphne waited patiently.
For him to return home to stay,
And never go away.
Daphne and Fred live next door.

Ruth Tickner, Guildford, Surrey

WOKING

From peacocks to aliens
Woking has it all
And we can certainly boast about
The best theatre of all

A beautiful park to wander through
Or take the kids to play
A leisure centre and a pool
To exercise each day

The area around the town
Is beautiful to see
With common land to wander on
Or have a picnic tea

In fact our town has everything
From racing cars to books
So come and visit us one day
Go on just take a look

You won't be disappointed
You'll want to dance and sing
We really are very proud
Of our town called Woking

Lynne Willis, Woking, Surrey

FRIMLEY

Frimley lives in Surrey County
Next to Camberley; their Surrey Heath.
In the high street filled with bounty
Restaurants, shops, banks; they are all a treat.

At the top of the hill stands St Peter's
A church with a square tower and no spire,
Some famous people are held in the graveyard
Even wood from HMS Victory is fashioned into a cross.

The Grove is of special interest
Not just because of grass and oak trees,
But a pound used in the medieval times
To hold animals that had gone astray.

Frimley Manor House is now a Cadet Centre
Where uniforms strut on parade,
The house and grounds stand to attention
A listed building, definitely top grade.

The White Hart commands attention
As it stands where three roads converge,
An ideal watering place for travellers
As it has been for many a long year.

Christine Evans, Frimley, Surrey

GUILDFORD THROUGH THE AGES

The Saxons first settled
Beside the River Wey,
The Normans came next
And were here to stay.

They built a castle
As a Royal abode,
Trading in blue cloth
Dyed with woad.

It was the obvious place
For a half way stop,
To rest the tired horses
And partake of a chop.

The barges carried goods
Up to London town,
Till the railway came
Bringing commuters down.

With a modern cathedral
And university too,
Shop till you drop
There's plenty to do.

Gillian Harris, Guildford, Surrey

THE SEASIDE WALKER

Bexhill promenade is such a delight
Seeing the flower beds so pretty and bright.

Passing the clock tower time to stop for tea
A glance at the De-la -Warr pavilion
Over looking the sea.

Then further along up galley hill
To view Eastbourne and Hastings coastal shores.
I wonder what more the future holds in store.

Valerie M. Bond, Bexhill-on-sea, Sussex

A GARDENERS DREAM - DAN DE LION

I was sitting in my garden
When a new plant I did spy
I can't believe I'd not seen it before
Because it really caught my eye
The flower was golden yellow
And the leaves an emerald green
I must confess that I thought
It was the best I've ever seen
And as I sat there looking
My joy I could not hide
It looked so good that when I stood
I just filled up with pride
That plant it was magnificent
And praise I did not need
When my neighbour Joe looked at me and said
Its just a blooming weed

Roy Ransom, Bexhill-on-Sea, Sussex

THE STRAND, BRIGHTON

When the evening turns silver and grey by the shore
And it's far enough distant to seem elegant, chic
Remember that familiar quaint sea-entranced pier?
Like the whisper of waves enticing with music.

When these sinuous waves may suffice for caress,
While the chug of a motorboat soothes like a plane
Ornamenting the skies on some jewelled afternoon,
As the sea-birds are clustering: cold striped grenadiers.

Or skiving, just dreaming on water, the mast of a ship
Points to yet one more timelessly ocean-spelled day,
As voluptuous waves whisper: nothing matters save this,
And that lemon sun hides in its curds and its whey.

Julie Whitby, Brighton, Sussex

Julie Whitby said: "My poetry has been published in numerous magazines and newspapers ranging from TLS, The Independent, The Scotsman to She, Ambit, Country Life, Poetry Review etc - most notably twenty one of my poems appeared in the Daily Express as their daily poem. My work has also featured in nine anthologies. A scholarship actress, I have twice read my poetry at the Voice Box Festival Hall, for the Brighton Festival and on the BBC. My first collection *The Violet Room* (Acunem Publications) and *Poems for Lovers* (Agenda Editions) can be ordered from bookshops."

RETIREMENT IN BEXHILL

"Bexhill is the place for retirement", they say.
How true. People come, and grow younger each day.
They walk by the sea or explore, in the car,
The historical sights and the gardens - not far
From lovely Bexhill.

The shopping is easy and friendly - no need
To rely on a car. Buy a trolley. Succeed
To wheel to your home ev'rything on your list.
And it acts like a zimmer to help you persist
In lovely Bexhill.

If theatre and music and art you desire,
The famous Pavilion gives all you require.
There are cafes and clubs and a new chance to learn.
Look no further for ideal retirement. Just turn
To lovely Bexhill.

Margaret K Brambleby, Bexhill-on-sea, Sussex

THE LOLLIPOP LADY

Our Lollipop lady makes her way
Down to the crossing once a day
The children streaming out from school
Stop at the kerb they know the rule
She keeps them all within her sight
They must not cross till the time is right
She looks at the traffic passing by
And judges it with practiced eye
Until she knows it's safe to go
Into the road and halt the flow
Stalwart in her place he stands
The childrens safety in her hands
Queen of the road for a minute or two
Until she lets the traffic through
So with the children safely gone
She smiles and waves the traffic on
her task is done she's on her way
All's well with her world for one day.

Grace Ball, Worthing, Sussex

BURGESS HILL

Burgess Hill is without doubt the nicest of towns,
Surrounded by fields, near the foot of the Downs,
The people are friendly, and welcome you there,
From the minute you move in, they show that they care.

If you want to buy clothes, or furniture, food,
They come to assist you - would never be rude.
The council works hard to keep everywhere smart
With walkways, and seats under trees - it has heart.

The schools and amenities are just so good
That people from outside all come in a flood.
There are banks, clubs, and churches to meet every need,
And parks where my daughter and I sit and read.

The trains go to London, and down to the coast,
And buses to all the outlying spots boast.
I like Burgress Hill with its friendly appeal,
And think that it certainly merits "Gold Seal".

Brenda Wymer, Hurstpierpoint, Sussex

SEA FRONT STROLL

Statue like on galley hill
Dismal is the imagery
Vague dreams and jumbled schemes
Churn behind tranquillity.
Traipsing over dampened ground
Blow and moisture bludgeoning
Clarify my clouded brain
Cutting, chill and freshening.
White caps out on channel ride
Frenzied for the pebbled shore
Crashing energies collide
Tumultuous their blended roar.
Light from cafe colonnade
Spills out over slickened path
Flying spume of salty spray
Fallout of the waves wrath.
Out along the west parade
Glimpses of a vernal sun
Tantalise through overcast
Has its course, the tempest run.

Andrew Carey, Bexhill-on-Sea, Sussex

OBJECTIONABLE CHANGES

The council decided to do away with the parking,
Which was conveniently situated in Devonshire Square
Although there's still a road running through it,
It's termed a piazza for flair
They have lined the sides of the road with concrete
Spheres,
Simply balls to you
Nobody seems impressed with this daft idea,
they're even talking of closing the loo
As Bexhill has an elderly population
And their bladders can be rather weak
What on earth do they expect them to do,
When they are dying to take a leak
No aspect of change has been for the better,
There are a lot of discontented folk
Any visitors to the town are so unimpressed,
They are constantly giving us a poke
The niceties have gone from our dear old town,
With no theatre or cinema open at present
So what do we do but just sit and stew,
As the changes we most certainly resent.

Peter Morris, Bexhill-on-Sea, Sussex

TRANQUILLITY

Let me take you by the hand,
And lead to you a place,
Where time stands still.
Where noise and bustle cease.
Just tranquillity, calm and peace.
The very thing most mankind craves.
You will find it in this place.
A place aptly named Peacehaven.
Situated on the south coast, between the south downs and
the sea.
You can walk along the cliffs and watch the changing tides.
Take a stroll upon the downs breathing fresh air.
Here you find no crowds to push and shove.
No shops, cafe's, nightclubs or the usual trappings found
in towns.
This is a place lost to time itself.
A place of family homes, peace and quiet.
An oasis in this world of stress, anxiety and rush.
Nothing disturbs Peacehaven on the south coast by the
sea.

Joan Iveson, Peacehaven, Sussex

MIDHURST

From the mists of time, it forged its' way,
The castle of St. Anne's Hill, ten sixty-six, didn't stay,
The Cowdray Mansion of fifteen twenty, stood proud,
The fire of seventeen ninety-three consumed it,
With mystery about,
Through the centuries, viscounts and earls,
Bohuns, Brownes and Pearsons, Midhursts' history whirls,
Early market traders, the dressmakers and tanners,
A mint for money, candle makers and sword makers,
The Spreadeagle and Angel Hotels, Coaching Inns, still
attest,
To bringing guests, tales of ghosts, royalty and rest,
The famous belong to Midhursts' tales,
Sir Charles Lyell, Mark Longhurst and H.G. Wells,
Gilbert Hannam, founded the Grammer School,
On Founders Day, gives a preacher, a pair of gloves, by
rule,
The Rother River gives way to Raft Races,
The Polo Matches, play at fast pace,
The Southern Railway, no longer there to chase,
Nestled within the Southdowns, sits beautiful Midhurst,
A town with grace, my choice, it's first.

Sherree Stringer, Midhurst, Sussex

BEXHILL

I live in Bexhill by the sea
A special place you must agree
A blend of buildings old and new
It's charms unique, and what a view
One sees from high up Galley Hill
A quiet spot one's heart to fill
At Hastings noise and folk abide
At Eastbourne, tourists side by side
But here one wonders leisurely
The parks, the beach with lots to see
The edifice with pride of place
The De la Warr so full of grace
And every year we all support
Our carnival, the queen, her court
And motor racing founded here
Parades along the front in gear
Good shops like Jaegers now no more
But charities gain by the score
Of course no place is perfect and
We too have eye sores wrongly planned.

Avice Land, Bexhill-on-Sea, Sussex

SUSSEX WOOD IN AUTUMN

Autumn climax of the year
Sum of all her richest moments
When trees stand rapt in consuming flame
What a clamour of colour
Glowing yellow, copper, red and gold.
Such utter loveliness
Ready for lavishing on the earth below
Bringing us, however briefly into joy
As we experience the artistry
And infinite variety of nature
In this flame-like wonder.

Idris Woodfield, Chichester, Sussex

BOGNOR REGIS

The king's alliteration made our town a joke
He poured contempt upon us even as he spoke
Nowadays - quizshows, - what's the booby prize
Fail to win the cruise on which you've set your eyes
A week in Bognor Regis is what they'll offer you
Just listen to the laughter amongst the camera crew
I know the town's old fashioned, the pier needs some repair
And for our needs the council do not seem to care
But, people are so friendly, new folk they will not shun
The weather's bright and breezy with loads of summer sun

Attractions are around us, all within our reach
If you feel adventurous, keen to leave the beach
Cathedrals, castles, houses, two racecourses too
You'll soon discover something you would like to do
So, come and stay in Bognor - never mind the jeers
I'm rooting for the Regis, giving it three cheers.

Muriel Sims, Bognor Regis, Sussex

158

HAMMERWOOD HOUSE

This really is my special place
I feel grand and full of grace,
As I sit on this garden wall
I feel quite rich, and ten feet tall,
Its so huge, and very bare
I imagine I am living there,
Something draws me back, most day's
It makes me sad, in many ways,
It needs a family, in this case
To fill this lovely lonely place,
I wonder what the history holds
For a house that is so old,
I don't think there were King's or Queen's
But uppercrust, it most certainly seems.
With servants, and a butler. to open the door
Onto a foyer, with a shiny floor,
The garden's need a gentle hand
To restore this lovely gracious land,
The house one day will be restored
And by many, be adored,
And then I am sure, that it will be
A special place for them, as well as me.

Susan Hoar, West Hoathly, Sussex

BLINDNESS

Many are the ways to help the blind,
From being a carer and getting around,
To making life easier, when its so hard,
Also by understanding those retired.

With many volunteers in our locality,
Some will run a group with versatility,
Others drive a minibus most days,
To local places and help in other ways.

With a hall nearby events take place,
One day will be art, later dominoes replace,
Another day a quiz or maybe a piano session,
So many can then relax after a fashion.

There are also for holiday inclined, a home,
Which basically serves all that maybe roam,
Her with aids for those partially sighted,
Life, can for a while, not be blighted.

So let us give praise for those great folk,
That give their time helping others cope,
With blessings from above to assist,
May those afflicted never need to desist.

William Burkitt, Hastings, Sussex

TWO UP, TWO DOWN

Two up, two down, the little cottage now
Stood clean, inviting, windows open wide;
A lady brought it, loved it; at the side
A gleaming greenhouse grew.

Together, she and home grew older, worn;
Her knees were stiff, and grey showed in her hair;
The paint peeled off, it looked unloved, forlorn;
The third step crumbled on the stair.

The weeds took over, smothering the bed;
The roses rambled freely to the sky;
Nettles and thistles grew around the shed
The hedge, uncut, obstructed passers-by

She went; the place was sold; a family moved in
(Two up, two down? How to accommodate that lot?)
They pulled the inside out (most went in the bin)
A digger dug the plot.

How sad a sight. A pretty, homely place
Harmonious with its neighbours now a block
Of soulless concrete, lacking charm or grace.
Two up, two down. Oh, please turn back the clock.

Katherine Daniel, Ninfield, Sussex

BEXHILL

Bexhill has many things,
That other towns do not.
Like the De La Warr Pavilion,
That stands by the sea in glory.
We have a clock tower that stands opposite our museum,
That's full of wonderful historic things.
The Manor Barn's where weddings are held,
And the sun beats down on beautiful gardens.
We also have the Highwoods,
Where you can stomp about in mud.
Our glorious beach gets lovely sun,
That brings everyone to the sea.
So all in all I hope you agree,
Bexhill is a wonderful place to be.

Olivia Baker, Bexhill-on-Sea, Sussex

CHRISTCHURCH

The priory bells rang out
Eight hundred years ago,
And then they rang on Sundays but
I didn't want to know.

I heard them ring in '58,
My marriage to proclaim;
However many times they ring
The call remains the same.

It says, "Come back again,
Come back and do not roam,
And when you hear the bells again,
You'll know that you are home".

Jacqueline Hitchen, Lindfield, Sussex

HASTINGS

King Harold at Battle in 1066
Beautiful countryside to add to the mix
The sunshine and seaside
A nudist beach too
These treasures of Hastings wait to welcome you.

The old town, All Saints
Stories of smugglers and rum
A trip down the caves
And to life, they do come
Yarns of old folklore, the Winchester gang
In those days in Hastings, it's said you could hang.

Ghostly appearances, old cobbled streets
Fish and chip restaurants around every street
Amusement arcades, White Rock Theatre, the pier
For the discerning tourist all this is here.

So come ye to Hastings
This place of my birth
And leave with a smile after holiday of mirth.

Antony May, St. Leonards-on-Sea, Sussex

*Dedicated to Margaret and Ian May, my parents. It's
because of your love that Hastings feels like home to me.*

BEXHILL BLARNEY

Now I'm older, not so spry
With fewer pleasures I can reach,
I sit and watch the world go by
Or search for treasures on the beach.

Every morning watch the dog
Sniff on line across the sward
Check the warning on his blog
On the canine message board.

The march of progress sometimes palls
And leads to irritation;
No parking, only Gubby's balls,
Beside the railway station.

Regeneration flats are due,
Rising up to heights obscene.
At least they'll have the perfect view
Across the rescued putting green.

Some days I grin, some days I shout
And watch my waistline fatten.
The tide comes in, the tide goes out;
All part of life's rich pattern.

Edward Breed, Bexhill-on-Sea, Sussex

NEWICK

Here stands amid the rolling weald,
Where sturdy oak spread thick,
Our ancient village on the green,
This Sussex scion, Newick.

No boastful claim does Newick make
To fame or notoriety,
Save of our annual Guy Fawkes night
And renowned bonfire society

Conserving cherished customs
These dedicated few
With pyrotechnic pageantry
Recall the failed coup.

Within our humble village hall
See N.A.D.S and reap rewards
Muse long, for here in former times
Did Bogarde tread these boards.

A brief glimpse of our village
Much more could be revealed
Of life in Newick on the green
Amid the rolling weald.

Roger Heath, Newick, Sussex

SUSSEX BY THE SEA

In Sussex there is a place that we
All know, where in later life we,
Seem to glow.

Retire, you say, not I
For at this later stage in my life,
I intend to reach the sky.

Drama, writing, painting is my theme
While my husband takes gardening,
With much enthusiasm or so it seems.

To spoil my grandchildren is my right
While at the beach,
Keeping them firmly within my sight.

After years of working with great skill
It's nice to relax at last and settle down,
With affection here in Bexhill.

Anne Whittington, Bexhill-on-Sea, Sussex

Born in Scotland, **Anne Whitington** has interests including writing and producing plays. "I joined writing classes to improve my writing and then I discovered that I had a talent for poetry," she explained. "My style flows from the heart and I would like to be remembered as a writer of good novels and poems." Aged 75, Anne is a housewife with an ambition to write a play and see it performed. She is married to Richard and they have four children. "The person I would most like to meet is the Queen because I admire her very much," added Anne.

IT'S A PROPER THING TO DO

I now have moved to Bexhill
I've always thought it true,
That as you reach retirement
It's the proper thing to do.

I love it here, it is so near,
To everything I need
Shopping, P. O., doctors too,
And a short walk to the sea.

It's quite an education,
Watching old folk get around
Manoeuvring those trolleys
To get their pension, they are bound.

Walking sticks and zimmer frames
Are the order of the day
They're going off to Sainsbury's
And they'll get there, come what may

So remember when you're getting on
If you want to feel at home
Come and live in Bexhill,
And you won't feel all alone.

Doris Sidders, Bexhill-on-Sea, Sussex

GLORIOUS GOODWOOD

Goodwood is a glorious place,
Of flashing silks and rolling hills,
Of Panama's and stripy ties
And taffeta, with lace and frills.

A lovely August afternoon,
With sunshine, bright and warm.
The grandstands full of glamour,
And ringing cheers, across the lawn.

But suddenly the brightness dims.
The favourite fails once more.
Although odds-on to win this race,
He struggles in; the last. of four.

Race on race are so exciting.
We try so hard to win the prize,
But the tipster's tips are failing fortune,
So chances fade, before our eyes.

At last we find a combination.
The jockeys good, on a hold-up horse.
He times his run to pure perfection.
Oh Goodwood; what a glorious course.

Dennis Harrison, Midhurst, Sussex

BEXHILL, PAST AND PRESENT

Lived in Bexhill all my life
Played upon the sand
Buildings along the prom
All so very grand.

The De-La-Warr was regal
Our town was so alive
It really makes me wonder
How long it can survive.

Open up the shops
Take the shutters down
Lets put the flags out
To salute our town.

Lets see the kiddies play
Ice cream in their hand
Then off to the park
To listen to the band.

So please one and all
Put on your coats and cap
Lets make our town the best
Put Bexhill on the map.

Jan Green, Bexhill-on-Sea, Sussex

OLD FLO

I'm sorry to see you go,
A fond farewell to ex neighbour Flo,
I'd heard the whispers, heard the talk,
But didn't believe you were going to York.

We both lived on Stifford for many a year,
Through lots of laughter, and many a tear,
Another eastender, to leave the east end,
Another goodbye to a very old friend.

They say you'll return in a couple of years,
I have my doubts, I have my fears,
They say out of sight means out of mind,
If you return, what will you find.

Stifford will be a building site,
Where to house you could be a plight,
Victoria Park is a very nice place,
For you to stay, for you to grace,
But if you find living in York is better,
Please don't forget to send me a letter.

Norman Sampson, Dagenham, Essex

CLACTON-ON-SEA

Clacton, my late discovered sweet Nirvana,
Quietly ensconced by the wild North Sea.
This mirco climate of exception
A long sought spiritual home to me.

Springtime flowers there and pendulous blossoms
Buoy the spirit, feed the soul.
The hovering kestrel along the sea front
Hunts below, the unwary vole.

The gentle landscapes soft undulation
Is kind to cyclists and those who walk.
At cafes when the day is clement
People come to sit and talk.

The town is a holiday trippers' mecca
Where sunshine seekers come and meet;
Sun bathing on the beach and swimming
Shopping in the lively street.

Photographing the rotating seasons,
Flora, fauna, whatever be;
Exploring hours in frost or sunshine,
Surprised in entrancing discovery.

Christopher Lane, Clacton-on-Sea, Essex

MY SALVATION

Holy Light fills thy chapel
We are given healing to the sickness as a curse
A cathedral of bells ring out thy truth
A faith that cares
A soul is filled with immaculate blessings
Clothe yourself with Christ's love
Evangelist Christian teachings we
Preach through our speech
Has your day been good or bad
Put punishment to shame
Believe in our holy Lord Jesus
Christ again

Antoinette Christine Cox, Basildon, Essex

CLACTON-ON-SEA

The seaside town hosts visitors from London
All they need for both holiday or home
A Riviera of the east coast that beckons
A sun dappled season of honeycomb
The pleasures, of sandy beaches, a busy town
Flower gardens where frail and elderly can sit
The wind down as mind, and body begins its slowdown
On deck chairs, benches drenched and sunlit
Clacton has charm and old time grace
Gentle winds with their tender fingers reach and warm
A little town, a nations showplace
That shelters from the stress of life's storms
To walk the seafront and amusement piers
The pinnacle of this lovely coastal sphere

Pamela Harris, Clacton-on-Sea, Essex

COLCHESTER

Roman Colchester is home to me
Full of interest for all to see,
The castle stands so proud and free
It's Roman bricks full of history.

A forward looking Essex town
With St Helena smiling as she looks down,
Thinking of visits there have been
From Boudicca, to our present queen.

Overlooking the river Colne
A Roman garrison town was born,
But Boudicca attacked them there
Causing destruction and despair.

Then during the English Civil war
We backed the losing side once more,
Colchester fell to Cromwell's men
With some royalists executed again.

Now Colchester is great for today
The oldest Roman town we say,
With outstanding schools leading the way
This modern Colchester is here to stay.

Christine Ward, Colchester, Essex

CHANGE

They are going to change old Wickford town,
Dress her up in a bright new gown.
But do we need a multiplex, or a Condominium?
It's just change for changes sake, if you want my opinion.

Once we had a cinema, was it called the Grand?
It was in the High Street just where Woolies stands
And did you know that, cattle once were washed in London
Road,
You know, by Bridge House Close, where the river
overflowed.

They'll demolish half of Southend Road, a massive
relocation,
Pedestrianise the High Street, and re-model the Railway
Station.
They'll be more Nail Bars, Tanning Shops and fast food for
our hunger,
But will their plans include a space for a decent
Ironmonger?

Can't they leave our town alone, all that mess, and dirt,
and dust.
It was good enough for our fathers, so it's good enough for
us.
They plan to spend a million, but I don't care what it cost,
As long as Mr Hall records it all, before our history it lost.

Ted Shirley, Wickford, Essex

DARTFORD

Growing up in Dartford, I was as happy as can be
Friendly shops and people were guaranteed you see
The park was full of magic for youngsters just like me
With swings and ponds with fish in and an ice cream or
cup of tea
The town was very busy and very safe to be
Not for us the nightclubs or the CCTV
We could go walking late into the night
Meet up with a friend or two with no thoughts other than a
nice night
I've watched the changes through the years, my head held
in my hands
No more walking in the street for any grans
Not for today's youngsters the magic of the park and trees
But I am very lucky for I have my memories
Of a happy, friendly Dartford I can share with my family

Sandra Leach, Dartford, Kent

BEXLEY BIRD

The dawn chorus of the little known Bexley borough bird
takes refuse in the sleeping heath.

His loyal family screech at his tail,
Resplendent in their brown, black and maroon plumage.

"Twit twoo, no sleep for you"
Pitch so high the glass is shattered,
The earth is moved.

The eagle-eyed hawk hovers overhead,
Surveying the burrow.

The sun comes out,
She smiles her radiant, golden smile,
Waves her royal hand,
Everyone sings a cheer.

Joan King, Welling, Kent

CAPEL HILL FARM

At Capel Hill at a place called Harty I could sit all day,
To watch the valley and the land beyond which seems so
far away.
I watch the cows and the sheep below, grazing by the fleet
and the scenery there is far beyond belief.
Looking to the river Swale, the sailing yachts pass by, and
cars and trains upon the mainland look like children's toys.
To our right, three prisons stand with about two thousand
men, and at night when all lit up looks like fairy land.
Beyond the prisons, the new Swale crossing high and so
erect spans across the isle to mainland, it's not finished
yet.
We've been told about the opening or what it will be called
But hopefully after an islander who has done good.
I wonder just how many years the views will stay like this,
The farm out there and the lights and sights to us, it's
heavenly bliss.

Daphne R Webb, Sheerness, Kent

MY LIFE ON SHEPPEY

Came to Sheppey from the north
to the south, met a bloke who
helped me out. Became a mate,
my husband too, we had three girls,
little boy too. Things got bad,
couldn't pull through. Got
depressed and even blue. Time
went past, couldn't pull myself
together, but got children
who love me forever. I was a
mess, took a house in Sheerness.
It did help me out without a
doubt, but glad of the move
that was a start. The smile
on our faces from the heart.
The man I met loves us
forever and that's made our
lives a long and lasting pleasure.

Lynn Capie, Sheerness, Kent

PEMBURY AT EARLY DAWN

Mid Pembury's blossoms at early dawn
Heralds the cuckoo's wakening call
And dew-soaked lawns like jewels do glisten
By phoebus early rays that's risen
Eftsoons the morning mist reveals
A landscape of beauty, vales and hills
Farms and orchards their fruit to bear
Their fragrance fills the rural air
Oast-houses standing from yesteryear
Memories of hop-picking and English beer
'Tis with much gladness and joy to recall
Mid Pembury's blossoms at early dawn

Terrence St John, Pembury, Kent

GILLINGHAM

As you drive down Ito way, look down upon the river
The sunshine gives it depth, the wind makes it quiver
Wildlife abounds there, look now and see
Birds fly back and forth enjoying being free

Your people need the freedom too, of safety, and thriving
shops
Give us back our Gillingham with loyalty that never stops
The town is our failing heart, so come, make it beat
Turn it into a welcoming place, and not a dead end street

The thriving Sunlight Centre, an excellent working scheme
Shows how dirty laundry, washes snow-white clean

Pamela Laflin, Gillingham, Kent

SIDCUP'S WORTH AND WELCOME

There is something about Sidcup
The people, the spirit, the fun
We are like a happy family up
The high street, spending our sum

No-one takes life too serious
For life is too short and too sweet
Well, perhaps only those delirious
Like binge-drinkers on the street

All things in moderation
Care and concern, don't ignore
We believe in the next generation
This one, and one before

So if you ever feel lonely
In need of a friend and the like
All you need do is only
Come to Sidcup, now, on your bike

Robert G Bedwell, Sidcup, Kent

CARNIVAL

Remember Mr Tollput
His horse-drawn set of wheels
Raucous tones, crying "rags, bottles and bones"
His black and white dog, a twirling
Ball of tail and heels?

Imagine if this cavalcade
Got mixed up with today's parade
As weekend visitors each Sunday night
Queuing for the exit as they jostle
And rumble up the hill
Bumper to bumper past that venerable old mill.

Then the off-roaders, mum in her four-by-four
Mopping up the kids from school, door-to-door.
Processing by the dozen, down
Streets that never change
With their curves and bends
The usual and the strange.
They'll hump whate're posterity sends
Whitstable's seaside carnival that never ends.

Gordon Brenchley, Whitstable, Kent

LIFE IN GRAVESEND

A simple scene, a busy street
Lots of places where people meet
Where else, I wonder, will you hear
The heart of Kent beat so clear?

From the Royal Terrace Pier you see ships go by
Carrying cargo for everyone to buy
Hanmer St, Parrock St, Windmill St, Milton Road
Contain many types of abode

Gordon Promenade
Really pleases you
Affording views too good to be true
Variety can be found at Woodville Halls
Either for parents or for schools
St George's Shopping Centre provides for us all
Either families large or families small
Near a church lies a girl of mystery
Dignified and known as Pochahontas in history

A town where different cultures blend
It can only be Gravesend!

Billy King, Northfleet, Kent

WESTERHAM

Hail, the greatest man in history
reclining in bronzed glory on Westerham green,
surrounded by whitewashed, Tudor beamed buildings
and serenaded by distant sirens on the "road to hell,"
as painted wrought iron invites you to take a seat,
relax and reflect with a tempting latte or mocha.

Nearby lies Chartwell, once home of the great man
who remains in the air with every breath we take.

Art Deco and posh frocks to fit stick insects
invite us to browse, while "Barely Read Books",
a tiny shop bulging with words and forgotten stories,
sits round the corner from an ancient church in a silent
graveyard,
with fallen stones and those who died too young.

So many restaurants, cafes, takeaways too, with leaned on
counters,
serve hungry customers watched quietly by the blackbird
who wishes for a fallen crumb as she sings her winter
song.

Patsy Goodsir, Westerham, Kent

SIDCUP

Many years ago I moved
From Essex down to Kent
And ever since, my married years
In Sidcup I have spent

In the High Street where the shops
That now exist no more
Cave Austin, Greigs, MacFisheries
Plus one department store

Time has changed suburban towns
Fast food and takeaways
Increasing traffic, causing jams
Restricted parking bays

Within a park there stands a school
That bears a well-known name
Where students of dramatic art
Begin their quest for fame

Some think the name of Sidcup odd
But who are they to say
For it has been immortalised
In Harold Pinter's play

Sheila J Leheup, Sidcup, Kent

THE LIBRARIAN

The librarian at my library,
Is very kind and polite,
She helps us find books,
And help us do our homework.

The Librarian at my library,
Is very positive about everything,
Ask them if you have a doubt,
Ask them right now!

Avin Philip, Ashford, Kent

NATURE'S GARDEN

Ambling gently come windswept
pastures embracing the
folds of ashen skies.
Nor wind, nor rain can
blemish this portrait, the essence of
England in nature's disguise.
The moan of cows and horses
slumber, amidst the chasms
of birds up high.
'Tis a rainbow's end
unveiling life cradled,
amongst the hills so
undefined.

Julie Fouad, Folkestone, Kent

ASHFORD

Now let us be wary of this obituary
We're not talking people born high
But more of a town that has been run down
That's bled its inhabitants dry.

The patient's not dead, just incredibly red
As folks all around do their nattering
The town has been fed and raises its head
To ask what the hell has been happening.

How do I pray find you today?
Perhaps somewhere between Cold and Embalming
Let us not say this place lost its way
But something much more alarming.

Now pour out a drink and let's have a think.
On how your size could be improved upon
It's swim or sink or that railway link
That surgeons are making a move on.

They've cut you up bad, it's terribly sad
But who's doing things to the letter
Your arteries cloggy and plans a bit foggy
I hope you're feeling much better.

Jessie Fisher, Ashford, Kent

DODE CHURCH

The little stone church is still standing
The only building to remain
Of the ancient village of Dode
Which had stood at the end of a country lane

History tells us the village did exist
Many years ago, bustling and alive
But the horror of the Black Death came
Wiped out the whole village, no-one to survive

The church became derelict, its stonework damaged
The object of vandals, their meeting place
But for a while the Church still used it
For services held on the Summer Solstice

Abused and abandoned, sold by the church
At last a new owner was found
The church was restored, inside and out
The grounds tended and fenced, made safe and sound

Today, Dode Church is a beautiful place
It stands mid green lawns, looked after and neat
Weddings are held here, and for those who seek solace
There has also been added a weekend retreat

Ann Harris, Rochester, Kent

RUSSIAN CANNON AT WELLING CORNER

I noticed you there all alone.
People pass by but you are still unknown.
In all weather, positioned on the Roman road facing up
Shooters Hill.
Due to a Royal Artillery Museum deal.

Similar to the Russian cannon used in the Crimean War.
A lot of killing from 1780 to 1860 saw.
Loaned by the museum in Woolwich.
For East Wickham became the ammunition workers home
pitch.

A Russian iron carronade 1854-56 thirty-six pounder.
Pride of place at Welling corner.
Calibre 6.75 inches, weight 17cwt.
Used to seal people's fate.

So next time you pass by me.
Feel free to stop and see.
Spend some time to ponder.
What happened yonder.

Research into the Great War history.
For you and for me.
So we never forget.
Those in the face of death.

Caroline D'Souza, Welling, Kent

FOOTSCRAY

I remember Footscray as a village with a row of quaint little shops
It even had an old water trough where you waited for buses to stop
Although Footscray was just a village, it had three pubs where you could go
The oldest was the Seven Stars, then the Red Lion and Barley Mow

People waited with anticipation for the annual show at Kolster Brands
With side shows, a fair, and fireworks, ending with dancing to local bands
Church fetes were held in the Old House, parties in the William Smith Memorial Hall
Once a circus came to the brick field where children enjoyed it all

Footscray had a village school, the clock tower showed if you were late
All Saints Church was just down the lane with its pretty lychwood gate
Beyond the church, the meadows, with the River Cray ambling by
Where once we stood and watched Footscray Place burn to ashes and finally die

Mary Millar, Sidcup, Kent

THE DARENTH VALLEY

Years beyond counting the earth's crust split
And created the valley, a rift deep and narrow
Where now is a village, a stream crept from the hills of
Westerham
To establish a swiftly flowing watercourse with kingcups
and reed beds

The village in the deep earth has a microclimate
And on a misty cold morning when the people shiver
If they climb the afforested sides of the valley
They might well find the warming sunshine

The frost lies late on the lush meadows in winter
The grass remains sparkling with dew from one day to
another
And the birds take refuge in the trees puffing out their
feathers
Only swooping down to pick up crumbs thrown from cot-
tage windows

The exploring Romans followed the then navigable river
And appreciating the fertile alluvial soil established their
settlements
Built their houses, raised their cattle, cultivated the fields
And planted their apple orchards

The pure waters of the Darenth were once used by paper
mills
To produce the finest writing paper
Alas, the mills have gone but the artist Samuel Palmer
painted here
And his work is famed and still much enjoyed

Brenda Gass, Shoreham, Kent

OUR HOME

Chiswick is home to me, familiar
As the flowers, the trees
A peaceful place I like to be
Many friendly people to talk to me
Many, many restaurants, seems the place to be
Down the high road people like to be
Customers sit under the tall, shady trees
A peaceful place they love to be
In the midst of Chiswick past
Hogarth painted works of art
In the sunlight I can see his
Little house where he used to be
I guess a place he loved like me
Outside the bank his statue stands
A pallet and paintbrush in his hand
A reminder of a life that's past
His gift to us, his works of art

Ann Smith, Chiswick, Greater London

PATRICIA THROUGH THE PILGRIM

Clouds burst
In the apple fields
The Stour Rose
HEr back turned
On a stool she sat
On the banks, on the banks
Behind bridges
Waiting
With
Healing hands
Touching the heart
Of the heart
In
Sole
Reflexes
Through the pilgrimage
At
The friends' meeting house

John Sheehy, Holloway, Greater London

SHOPKEEPER'S ALLEYWAY

At the end of our street there is an alleyway
With rubbish piled up high, the smell
Would ruin your day
Discarded cans and boxes and empty
Bottles of beer, day after day, more rubbish
Seems to appear
Fly tippers tip their rubbish then tip-toe away
They must be dumping at night time there
Never to be seen by day
Now that it's all cleared up, we're hoping
It stays that way
So as to walk down our street
And never let it spoil the day

Paul Andrew Newman, Brockley, Greater London

DOWN THE ROAD APIECE

It's just a street
Sometimes so quiet
Sometimes alive
With the sound of children's laughter
Where neighbours walking dogs
Pause to speak
Comparing notes on dogs and shops
And the ever fickle weather,
And for a moment time stands still,
Then a baby cries
So, on we go
Towards another day
In this sometime quiet street
But sometimes alive with sound

Margaret Freeman, South Harrow, Greater London

CALLING OLD CROYDON

The streets aren't the same anymore
Shiny new buildings, central's new stores
Mirroring blessings of times gone by
Deflecting the noise of a young girl's cry
Shadows are cast now on many men's faces
Murder, rape in quiet spaces
Children are bullied so bullies they become
Filming beatings as happy slap fun
Madness rises like a red sea in Egypt
Awaiting a Moses MP to recede it
Dirty needles mistaken for toys
A rise in drug addict girls and boys
A* - C grades sit in pockets
As uni places plummet and unemployment rockets
Police suppose a protective presence
Everyone scarred from July seventh
Crush the new and bring back the old
Where women are safe and children do as they're told

Gailann Houston, Croydon, Greater London

THE STREETS

The locals here are ghosts
Their tamarind skin glows transparent
And they roam with dark faces
They are sick with oppression
They do not smile at the post office
They drawl in their Sylheti accents
About home, they want to go back home
Where the grass is greener than Mile End's park
And herds cause the only traffic
These locals are unhappy creatures
Old and weary, the old generation are coming to pass
And I see the new locals
Crack at the canals
Weed at the street corners
Heroin at the local travel stations
These dealers are blurring
And I'm the lingerer to stand
And watch this place go downhill

Rumi Begum, Greater London

THE BOY IN THE HIGH STREET

A thin frame crouched in a doorway
Breathing on his chapped hands, trying to keep warm
Dishevelled clothes terribly tattered and torn
Old trainers full of holes
Let in the wet, no escape from the cold
Poor forgotten soul
You can see a world of pain behind his baby blue eyes
Desperate and forlorn, but you'll never see him cry
He's made a sign, it reads, hungry and homeless
Wealth walks by uncaring and blind
Contemptible stares as if he's committing a crime
I give him some change, it's all I can spare
In the city of London a child is begging
Doesn't anybody care?
With a swift glance he looks up, his being so incomplete
He smiles, slowly nods, then goes back to gazing at the
street
In the western world they claim we are poverty free
But some streets in London, poverty is all that you'll see

Jackie Nicholson, Chingford, Greater London

A TOWN

On Monday morning beer is brewed,
It smells like strong tea,
And wafts into the atmosphere;
Tower blocks pierce the solemn sky,
All areas of green have been swallowed
By a concrete wasteland,
Litter strewns the streets,
Decayed houses stand forlorn by the quayside,
And the river is choked with oil and weeds.

Ebony clouds hover in the air,
Factory chimneys excrete black fumes,
Houses have been painted with soot,
People struggle to walk on cracked paving stones,
A woman trips and falls,
When she rises from the pavement she limps,
Everyone ignores her 'though she looks in pain,
She waits for a bus to take her home,
It arrives an hour later,
And crawls through the dismal streets.

Sarah Sidibeh, London

SUN SETTING ON IALOMITZA RIVER

Again light slips out of my eyes and I feel about like a
blind,
my body unscrolls over things it cannot see.
Forever in motion, listless as I'm made of many grains, it's
their intensity
that carves these banks so they'll hold more of me.

However my grains mix, tenderness will always be in them.
Day gets suspended like scales between the rooms of my
heart;
only when sky is red am I at stand still. It is then when
I don't remember your words, but I remember all your
silences,
hear them from under nine layers of birds.

And I learn how to dance in the blood of my heart.
When the gate behind is closing, I start to move across the
waters,
my body drowning, but my love keeping afloat.
I remain a lover in the tomb of my heart.
With me goes the sound of gulls.

Elena Tincu-Straton, Greater London

198

LET'S SET SAIL FOR COLINDALE

Welcome to my home where life is great
The flats are bordered with a cold, metal, green gate
To some the area is a priceless piece of art and should be
hung in the Tate
Others want it knocked down, hung and can't wait for that
date

This is the place full of car showrooms and we have our
own underground station
Bus routes, taxi ranks, cycle lanes and a representation of
different nations
There are Hindus, Jews, Muslims, Christians and even
Pagans
Just a place north-west of London is the location

There are millionaires and murderers that could tell a
Knight's tale
We've got winners, losers, those that succeed and those
that fail
Whether looking for some groceries or on search for the
Holy Grail
Let's set sail for Colindale

Dipesh Tailor, Colindale, Greater London

NEIGHBOURHOOD PLAGUE

Ring at the bell, impatient, knocking wild
It's old nosey parker with a cuppa in her hand,
"I'm not one to gossip but them across the way
Music blaring all night long, like a percussion band!"

Telephone shrieking, it's Beth on the line
"Had a letter of complaint re the litter in my drive."
"Been round to nosey parker to find out what's the matter
Wasn't her, it's them across the way.
She heard them having a natter."

Knock at the door, its the RSPCA
"You're hound's not walked, your cat's not splayed
We're taking them away."
Round to nosey parker, confrontation's on its way.

See old nosey parker, eyes blank, nose pressed against the pane
Quietly contemplating who's next for the frame.
Wasn't her, she knows nought, never one to complain.
Another day, another year, and there she goes all alone
Poor old nosey parker shuffling down the lane.

Susan Vango, Isleworth, Greater London

THE HOME ON THE HILL

High on the hill there stands a place
Whose doors will never close
On those who need a smiling face
And succour and repose

The Thames flows softly there below
And Petersham Fields are spread
Rear windows catch the sunset's glow
To bathe each chair and bed

Some do not know what days or years
Slip silently away
They cannot share their smiles or tears
As we, the lucky may

We owe so much to young and old
Who pass within these walls
Support to keep them in the fold
Find answer to their calls

Now through the quiet corridors
Another army treads
The carers and the comforters
The makers of the beds

So when the poppies all have gone
And winter winds grow chill
Remember those who soldier on
In that Home upon the Hill

Peggy Day, Ashford, Greater London

COBHAM

When you drop an "h" in Chobham
You will spell the name of Cobham
Which in fifty years for me has been the tops
So it's really not surprising
That the house's price is rising
Being near to the supermarkets and the shops
With a choice of churches, halls and pubs
A host of varied sporting clubs
Including Probus if retired
A water mill to be admired
Bank holidays are very grand
We even have our own brass band
If Cobham Players have no show
Then Painshill Park's not far to go
If overseas you have to go
You're close to Gatwick and Heathrow
Plus trains to London or a drive
But use A3 not 25
For full reports and people's views
Be sure to read the "Cobham News"

Peter J Marsh, Cobham, Surrey

MAYBE IT'S BECAUSE I'M A LONDONER

Life in London, where Londoners unite
When things get bad we put up a fight
Black, white, chinese or asian we stand together tall
Every race religion equal, everybody big or small
Our air may be smelly, we don't like to walk
We use our cars far too much, use slang when we talk
We like to live on fast food, we watch too many soaps
Spend far too much time down the pub, telling dirty jokes
But we all come together when we know there's a need
We're serious, we're focused, our decisions agreed
Our London is not perfect, but to be a Londoner is neat
And when the government annoys us,
You'll find us outside Downing Street.

Tarnya Glover, Thornton Heath, Surrey

OF CITY NOTE

I find a symphony pervades
Each quarter of metropolis;
Melodic movement, subtle shades
Charm, daily I'm aware of this;
Not only chords in Fairfield Halls
Inertia urban, dull beguile,
But marketeer repeated calls
Make rhythmical the shopping mile
Where busker poignantly performs
Prays discover, oh discover me.
His soul laid bare to city swarms,
Appreciative yet fancy free.
Croydon's own orchestral numbers,
Its vivid voices cheating time,
Here that maestro seldom slumbers,
Historic clock tower's mellow chime.
Bewitched I'm fired with civic pride,
Attuned, alert to vibrant metre,
Sounds sentimental where abide
Folk finding theme grows ever sweeter.

Ruth Daviat, Croydon, Surrey

A LAST JOURNEY

The railway man from Woking Homes
Would shuffle gamely into town,
Along the busy street.

With weathered face and toothless grin
His working days long over now,
He is a joy to meet.

Do you recall how Paddy stood
Outside a barber's shop one day,
His riddles always neat.

The road has changed since last we met;
The council put new paving slabs
And has removed the seat.

The chain not for improper use
And scarlet bell pull by the bed,
Hang idly in the heat.

When I must join the thronging crowd
At Peter's pearly barrier,
Will he be there to greet?

David Pennant, Woking, Surrey